EVERY WOMAN'S
GUIDE TO INVESTING

EVERY WOMAN'S GUIDE TO INVESTING

11 Steps to Financial Independence and Security

FRANCIE PRINCE

AND

DOUGLAS NOLAN PI

PRIMA PUBLISHING

PRIMA PUBLISHING and colophon are trademarks of Prima Communications, Inc.

Investment decisions have certain inherent risks. Prima therefore disclaims any warranties or representations, whether express or implied, concerning the accuracy or completeness of the information or advice contained in this book. Any investments a reader may make based on such information is at the reader's sole risk. You should carefully research or consult a qualified financial advisor before making any particular investment.

Library of Congress Cataloging-in-Publication Data

Prince, Francie.
  Every woman's guide to investing: 11 steps to financial
independence and security / by Francie Prince and Douglas Pi.
      p.   cm.
  Includes bibliographical references and index.
  ISBN 0-7615-0285-8
    1. Women—Finance, Personal.   2. Investments.
  I. Pi, Douglas.   II. Title.
HG179.P367   1996
332.6'082—dc20   95-36031
                                                                CIP

96 97 98 99 AA 10 9 8 7 6 5 4 3 2 1

Printed in the United States of America

How to Order:
Single copies may be ordered from Prima Publishing, P.O. Box 1260BK, Rocklin, CA 95677; telephone (916) 632-4400. Quantity discounts are also available. On your letterhead, include information concerning the intended use of the books and the number of books you wish to purchase.

CONTENTS

ACKNOWLEDGMENTS

D oug and I would like to thank some special people who have helped us with this book. We would like to acknowledge Donna and Barry Render for taking the time to read, edit, and format our proposal. Without their assistance, we would not have known how to get started. We also want to thank my design partner, Mark Mueller, for always being available to edit or type the manuscript or carry the work load at the office so that I could complete this project.

We would also like to acknowledge our agent, Jackie Simenaur, for taking a chance on "first-time" authors and successfully marketing our book to a very insightful and talented editor at Prima Publishing, Georgia Hughes, who helped mold the book. Her input and direction have been invaluable. We want to recognize Susan Silva, our project editor, who has been a tremendous asset to the book. She has made what might have been a difficult task, a joy.

There are many people in the investment field who have volunteered their time and vast knowledge to help our book be the best on the market. Mary-Lee Carey spent considerable time with us, making sure we had the most accurate information available on retirement planning. The highly respected economist, Bill Helman, allowed us to reproduce his proprietary *Monetary Pressure Index*—a fundamental ingredient in our investment philosophy. Alan Shaw, one of Wall Street's most esteemed technicians, permitted us to use some of his technical information in our chapter on picking stocks. Richard McDermitt was also helpful in the technical area. He allowed us to use his charts of Magee and Edwards, masters in the field of technical analysis. Steven Sciarretta was a tremendous help in the area of estate planning.

A special thank you goes to Marileigh Hensley and Doug VanScoy for realizing the need for *Every Woman's Guide to Investing* and helping wherever and whenever possible.

We would like to thank our parents, family, and friends for believing in us. I want to thank my daughter, Courtney, for her love, encouragement, and support. Doug wants to acknowledge the late Irving Goldman and A.A. Gentile—two demanding and astute investors who believed in him before he learned to believe in himself. We are grateful to all of these people, without whom this book would never have been possible.

EVERY WOMAN'S GUIDE TO INVESTING

INTRODUCTION

"[Every day, try to] do something foolish, something creative and something generous."

—BENJAMIN GRAHAM

Doug Pi dashed through the door of the airplane just before the stewardess closed the hatch. Out of breath, he found his seat, snapped his seat belt into place, and settled in for the long flight from New York City to Melbourne, Florida. Today he needed that time to sort through the myriad of feelings that crowded his thoughts. He had just come from the funeral of a revered friend and mentor, Tony Bocelli. Doug was a stock and commodities broker, and Tony had shown unwavering support over the years—in fact, he gave Doug his first big stock order. Tony represented everything that was good and positive about Wall Street.

Doug's client was from the "old school." He believed that finances were the man's responsibility, and he had successfully amassed a considerable fortune. The problem that nagged at Doug now was that Tony had left behind a wife and two adult daughters who were unaware of his financial status. He had prepared his family only by telling them that they could trust Doug. Doug had always had the support of his clients. Because of that support, he felt an intense sense of responsibility to protect their investments.

Now the burden was on Doug to educate Tony's family. Doug had been in the business for fifteen years and dealt with some of the country's most wealthy and famous personalities, and this lack of involvement by many women regarding their family finances had become a recurring problem.

Doug and I have been friends for several years, ever since I redecorated his beach residence in Melbourne, Florida. I am a successful interior designer. I own my own business and have a master's degree in interior design. On one occasion, Doug asked me what I knew about investments. Other than money market accounts and certificates of deposit, the extent of my investments was one venture. When I was eight years old, my father decided that it was time to teach my brother and me about the stock market. He took fifty dollars from our savings accounts and bought Holiday Inn stock for us. Holiday Inn was a new and growing company at the time, and he felt it would be an exciting one to watch.

My father drew a chart for us to log the stock's ascent, mounted it on the wall, taught us how to follow "our" stock in the newspaper, and we were off. I was very young, and the details escape me, but I remember watching my new investment go down every day for a couple of weeks. I wanted a quick return. My dad did not want to sour me on the market, so he bought back my stock for what I paid for it. He watched the stock skyrocket and split many times over the years. He even went on to build and own several Holiday Inns himself. I did not grasp investing principles at the age of eight, and I had come no further over the last thirty-four years.

My childish beliefs can be compared to those of many women. We want a quick fix, and if we do not get it, we will let the men invest because we believe they understand the markets. Doug found this alarming. Some of his most astute investors were women, but he admitted there was often a learning curve involved in getting them up to speed. So, he decided to explain the markets to me in a way that was comprehensive and interesting so that together we could educate others.

After much research and investigation, we discovered that there was no such training tool available—that covered everything and was easily understood by a novice yet could also challenge a sophisticated investor. Since wealthy people get their information from sources unavailable to the general public, we wrote *Every Woman's Guide to Investing* to educate Doug's female clients and make the secrets and investment techniques of the nation's most affluent accessible to all. This is *not* a financial planning manual, but rather a logical progression of steps toward building financial security. It explains investing while also exposing the problems and pitfalls that exist for women on Wall Street.

Investment professionals do not treat women the same way that they treat men. Various studies have been conducted by *Money* magazine to determine if financial advice is sexist. The studies found the following:

1. Female investors were taken less seriously than male investors.

2. Sales representatives offered women less assistance and pursued their business less aggressively.

3. Brokers spent an average of nine minutes longer interviewing male clients than female ones.

4. Brokers mentioned more diverse groups of investments to men. They mentioned four items to men but only three to women, individual stocks 58 percent of the time to men versus 34 percent of the time to women, mutual funds first to 80 percent of women versus 64 percent for the men, and brokers gave men recommendations for higher risk, higher return items.

Seventy-nine percent of the brokers interviewed were men; therefore, it is not possible to determine from the studies if female brokers treat women clients differently than male brokers do.

Please do not misconstrue this information. To give an example: a woman, Mrs. Jones, called a local brokerage office and specifically requested an appointment with a female broker because of the study conducted by *Money* magazine. The branch manager explained to the caller that their only female broker, Susan, would be out of the office for the next nine days. Mrs. Jones agreed to wait for Susan's return. As it happened, the client had $500,000 to invest, but the firm's only female broker was a rookie with less than one year of working experience and *no* experience handling an account of this magnitude.

The bottom line is if you are going to pick a broker, do not base your decision on the broker's gender; rather, select the person who is best qualified to handle your account.

Another interesting finding was that women themselves often feel inadequate about investing and making financial decisions. A study conducted by the Boston money management firm Liberty Financial found that the confidence gap starts early and is not limited to just older and middle-aged women. They surveyed junior high school students and found that the male students were almost twice as likely as females to view themselves as "very knowledgeable" about money and investments. Interestingly enough, Liberty Financial's study found there was actually little difference between the knowledge of the males and females.

Another endorsement for female investors is investment clubs. All-female clubs perform best of all, with a lifetime earnings rate of 10.2 percent, compared to 8.7 percent for all-male groups and 9.96 percent for mixed-gender groups. Since 1981, the National Association of Investment Club's 2,000 all-female clubs have outperformed the 2,900 all-male clubs in seven out of the eleven years. There is much speculation on why this is true. Some believe that women tend to do more research and then to hang on for the long haul. Research has shown that women do not let their egos get in the way of making a profit—they do not feel the need to "beat" the Dow or to be "right" just for the thrill of being right. Women just want to make money while avoiding unnecessary risks. They tend to save for specific goals and want long-term investments.

Regardless of your reasons for buying this book, it is time for women to get accurate, well-organized information in a format that peels away the Wall Street jargon and explains investing in plain and simple terms. For the first time here is a book on investing, written for women, that unravels the mysteries of Wall Street while preparing women for any situation that might arise. After following the steps set forth in *Every Woman's Guide to Investing*, you too can achieve financial independence and security.

STEP I

DEVELOPING A FOCUS

"Nothing is particularly hard if you divide it into small jobs."

—*HENRY FORD*

Highly successful individuals always maintain a finely honed focus. They develop a discipline that is consistent and clear. After spending the last fifteen years working for some of the nation's wealthiest and most successful people, we discovered that there were similarities in the approaches of the wealthy, regardless of the venture. Wealthy people all have certain things in common: a way of looking at complicated material in an organized yet simplified manner.

Investing changes the way you look at everything. Your thought process begins to evolve. You begin to develop a clearly defined focus: to become financially independent. If you read and view the material in this book from the standpoint of becoming financially independent and secure, you

7

too will develop a clear focus, and the material will fall into place for you.

Almost every business is and always has been affected by swings in the economy, but the difference is that you will become aware of this. As you go through the chapters of this book, you will begin to look at common occurrences differently. If you never watch *Wall Street Week* on public television or CNBC on cable television because most of it makes no sense to you and the rest just does not interest you, this will change. Soon you will understand it and find it fascinating.

Women need to take proactive positions where their financial futures are concerned. A good place to begin is by developing an awareness of common economic activity. There are many ways for even a novice investor to observe the economic climate. You must have faith that you can determine the best time to buy and sell stocks and bonds. Watch for signals, learn to think independently, and have confidence in your decisions. For example, the next time you go shopping and there are great sales in progress (because you now have a firmly entrenched focus on becoming financially independent), do not just think about how great it is that there are bargains to be had—look deeper and think that perhaps there is an oversupply of merchandise on the market and try to figure out how this will impact you and your family in your businesses and lifestyle.

If you go to your favorite restaurant, and it is empty several Saturday nights in a row and no other circumstances have changed (for example, a new restaurant did not open across the street and the quality of the food did not deteriorate), enjoy the solitude and start thinking about which stocks and bonds to purchase. If a normally busy restaurant is empty, people probably are cutting back on their spending. The economy is slow. The best time to buy stocks is in the middle of a recession.

Go to the mall on a major shopping day. If it is uncrowded and there are plenty of parking spaces, locate the stores that are busy and find out if their stock is publicly traded. Stock in these stores may be good to own. If the mall is busy, consumer spending may be up, and the Federal Reserve might be getting ready to raise interest rates, so this might be a dangerous time to purchase stocks and bonds. Look further.

Ask Realtors about their sales. If business is slow, financial markets are probably sound. If Realtors are busy and selling a lot, money may be going into real estate and housing, and again interest rates could rise. These are signals to check further.

Talk with your interior designer. If business is good, it could be a sign that the economy is strong. If it is too strong, interest rates will go up, and that could hurt the stock and bond market.

Look at car dealer advertisements. If dealers offer excellent finance rates, the demand for their product is weak. Bonds love misery. If the economy is slow and people are out of work, bonds do their best. Bond prices generally move ahead of stocks. If the bond market is strong, a strong stock market will usually follow. A slow-growing, steady economy is ideal for stocks and bonds.

Check on brokerage stocks such as Merrill Lynch, Legg Mason, or Charles Schwab. These stocks are usually among the first to turn up in a bull market. A *bull market* is an upward-trending market. A *bear market* is a downward-trending market.

If you notice any of these signs in either direction, check Federal Reserve activity. The Federal Reserve acts to control the demand for money by raising or lowering the cost of money or interest rates. When the Federal Reserve lowers the discount rate, it is encouraging banks, corporations, municipalities, and individuals to borrow money and to spend in order to stimulate the economy. The discount rate is the rate "the Fed" charges banks to borrow money.

When the Federal Reserve lowers the discount rate, the signal is to buy stocks and bonds. Lowering discount rates usually brings about favorable conditions that hold for a while. When it raises the discount rate, the Federal Reserve has decided that the economy is growing too fast, and raising the discount rate is how it applies the brakes.

The majority of people on Wall Street disregard these basic rules and act only on the basis of emotion. Ego and emotion can be the root of many problems for investors. We have found that women are less prone to the problem of ego than men. Women care more about making money than about just being "right." If you have this attitude, it works in your favor and can make you a better investor. The best you can hope to be is a student of the markets, as there are always new things to learn.

Determining economic trends may, at first, seem impossible to you, but you are actually observing them every day. Spotting trends is merely a matter of reprocessing common information. If all of this still seems a little confusing, do not feel concerned. By the time you finish this book, all the pieces will slip into place. The first step to confidence and financial independence will come with developing your focus, then with understanding the information and terminology, and finally with knowing how to pick the appropriate advisor for your investment needs.

Every Woman's Guide to Investing will give you a usable discipline that will allow you to first preserve capital and reduce risk and then achieve a reasonable return on your investments. We have broken the investment process down to eleven steps—each one building on the last. If you follow the steps listed in this book, you will learn how to make money over the long term and reduce your risk of losses.

The investment discipline outlined herein is not the *only* one that works, but it has worked successfully for many investors. In today's world of computers and technology, we are bombarded with information on investing. There are television channels devoted only to the news, the economy, and investing. In the search for the "hot" story or the latest "merger" or "buyout," we often are forced to suffer through hours of a television commentator's prattle that serves only to fill the air time. One has to have a method to sort through all of the available information to arrive at the crux of each issue. The ability to develop a clear focus is a must. The wealthiest client of one successful broker has said that if he had one bit of advice, it would be to never take your eye off the ball. In investing, this involves learning to concentrate on the basics. You will learn to study the effects of interest rates on stocks and bonds, supply and demand, leverage, cash flow, and market psychology before participating in any investment.

Breaking investing down to eleven steps simplifies the process. The first step, developing a focus, is the foundation of the investing formula. It involves learning a new way of thinking that cuts through all of the unnecessary material and allows you to evaluate opportunities in a simple way. The country's most successful investors all seem to have that clear, well-developed focus, and they all look for opportunities where no one else is looking. They listen to everyone, but then count on themselves. Extremely wealthy people do not have an agenda. They do not have to own something because everyone else owns it, *and* they have the tolerance to let opportunities pass in order to be selective. They also have the patience to wait for other investors to make mistakes. They know that if they wait long enough, everyone will eventually make a mistake, and they are ready and waiting to capitalize on the errors of others. When they buy, they know all of the essential ingredients are present and in the correct amounts. When asked if he was a buyer of a particular item, one of New York's wealthiest individuals stated, "I'm a buyer of all items . . . but at the right price."

A successful commodity broker schooled others in the art of trading commodities by explaining the value of patience. He told a fellow broker that investors should make every decision with the utmost caution. They should limit the number of commodity trades to five a year and not make the sixth trade even if someone put a gun to their

head. If you approach investing from this view-
point, you will carefully analyze each decision and
look at everything that can possibly go wrong. You
will also not be afraid to miss an opportunity,
because you know that there will always be other
opportunities. Successful people know that they
need not do every deal, so they choose the best
opportunities and then buy as much as they
can afford.

When analyzing similarities among wealthy
investors, one realizes that most of them have
many attributes in common, regardless of their
particular investment styles. By examining these
similarities, we can enhance our likelihood for success in achieving our investment focus. The most
prosperous clients all have plans and goals and are
persistent in their drive to achieve. None would
ever take the time to dwell on successes or failures.
They are like sponges, absorbing all the information that they can accumulate, and listening, not
talking. They surround themselves with the most
knowledgeable people they can find. Henry Ford
once explained this concept by saying that he did
not have to know everything himself, but he knew
where to get the information at the touch of a but-
ton. For example, one wealthy client is a young,
self-made man who does not handle investing personally but has chosen to delegate that responsibility, because his time is better spent focused on
his way of making money. If you choose this path,
be sure to delegate wisely.

When investing, effective speculators always
look at all sides of every deal. The first thing they
want to know is what can go wrong; then they look
for the opportunities. The trends and themes in

the markets cause shifts and show when to enter or exit. Prosperous investors study the behavior of other investors and the psychology of the market. They are all risk takers . . . but in these cases, the risks are calculated risks.

There was another interesting similarity that surfaced, while analyzing wealthy investors. Each of these successful people had a strong code of ethics. All were spiritually connected and huge financial contributors to their faith. Although the particular religions varied, the constant was that these people all believed in a higher power, and their spirituality made them humble. Many worthwhile philanthropic endeavors have been funded by these individuals. There is a responsibility that accompanies vast wealth, and the majority of the moneyed live up to that challenge.

This probably sounds like an overwhelming amount of information to understand and master, but if you take it a step at a time, your knowledge base will grow and develop. Each step builds logically on the next. This book contains only eleven steps, and you can take your time with each one until you feel comfortable and ready to proceed. You have already completed your first step to financial independence and security. Before we move on to the next step, "Understanding the Foundation," let's review.

SUMMARY

- Learn to develop and maintain a consistent and clear focus.

- Become aware of the economic environment and learn to spot trends.
- Learn patience in investing.
- Study the habits of successful investors and make them your own.

There are eleven steps to this investing discipline. Learning these steps will enable you to achieve financial independence and security.

STEP II

UNDERSTANDING THE FOUNDATION

"If money be not thy servant, it will be thy master."
—SEVENTEENTH-CENTURY PROVERB

T he women were all seated when the last stragglers entered the room and settled into the available chairs. It was a very diverse group—some young and still in college, some old and frail, many in the prime of their lives. But, there was a common bond that tied them together. They were all members of a private women's organization—a philanthropic, educational organization established for the betterment of women. At every meeting there is always a presentation, and each member is responsible for giving one from time to time. Today's topic was "Financial Awareness."

According to the IRS, nearly 42 percent of households with assets of $600,000 or more are headed by women. An unsettling fact is that all marriages end—50 percent end in divorce, and 70 percent of the rest end in the death of the husband. Therefore, nine out of ten American women are expected to be in charge of their finances at one time or another.

All one had to do was look around the room to realize that these statistics were accurate. The membership was composed of widows, career women, some divorcees, and some single women. The presentation was given by a woman who taught finance courses at the state university and wanted to give her club members a broad overview of financial markets. While waiting for the presentation to begin, comments such as "I don't know anything about finances—my husband takes care of all of that for me," "Financial programs bore me to tears. I generally tune them out," and "Perhaps I will learn something from this program . . . she appears to have achieved financial security" could be heard.

You too may have shared these sentiments, but now recognize the need to realize your goals and become financially independent.

Before a novice can learn about investing, there are some unfamiliar terms that need to be understood. Be aware that people on Wall Street seem to speak a foreign language. The following account emphasizes this point.

Kelly had just returned from a meeting with her broker. She and her husband had had several of these meetings because they were reviewing various money managers and their styles. Her broker kept mentioning "growth managers" and "value managers." Afterward, Kelly, an attorney with a degree in psychology, asked a friend what these terms meant. The pertinent issue is why she did not ask the broker to define these terms. Why was she uncomfortable asking questions of her broker? If you feel it is either an imposition or embarrassing to ask your broker questions, you may have the wrong broker. The point to stress here is to ask questions if there is something that you do not understand and keep asking until you feel comfortable with the material.

Before you can make intelligent decisions about which investments are right for you, you must first understand the basic theories and terminology. This chapter defines many investment terms. It explains different investment options in an elementary manner and tells you where you can find more in-depth information on each investment. If your broker suggests that you purchase intermediate-term securities such as U.S. treasury notes, you can look up U.S. treasury notes in this chapter and then flip to the section of the book on debt instruments to get a more in-depth explanation. Once the terminology is clear, the fundamental theories are easy to grasp.

To begin, there are only three ways to make money on your investments:

1. By earning interest or dividends on the investment.

2. By appreciation of the investment itself.

3. Through a combination of the two known as *total return.*

The only reason we invest is to make money, so let's see what opportunities are available and figure out the best possibilities for you.

TWO TYPES OF INVESTMENTS

There are only two types of investments. Investments are either equity (owner) or debt (loaner) investments. So, if you invest, you are either an owner or a loaner.

Owner Investments

Owner investments are stocks, either common stock or preferred stock. When you buy a stock, you buy a piece of the company. Historically, stocks have proven to be the best investment. The primary reason for buying a stock is capital appreciation. Capital appreciation means that the value of the shares is increasing.

When you talk about the stock market, you are generally referring to common stock. Common stock may or may not pay a dividend. A dividend is the portion of earnings that a company pays out to its stockholders. The other variety of stock, less commonly held, is preferred stock. Preferred stock will be discussed only briefly in this book. Preferred stock has reduced risk but also limited returns. Its dividend is paid before the common stock dividend. It is more costly than common stock, but it has a more secure dividend. In the

Investment Options

Owner Investments	Loaner Investments
	Taxable
Common Stock	U.S. treasury bills
Preferred Stock	U.S. treasury notes
	U.S. treasury bonds
	Zero coupon bonds
	Government agency bonds
	Corporate bonds
	Nontaxable
	Municipal bonds

event of bankruptcy, preferred stockholders are paid before common stockholders.

Loaner Investments

With debt (or loaner) investments, you loan your money to someone else, such as the U.S. government, a corporation, or a city, and they pay you interest for the use of your money at a pre-determined amount and for a predetermined time period. Debt investments, or instruments, fall into two categories—taxable and nontaxable. Taxable income instruments will be examined first. (U.S. treasury bills, notes, and bonds are taxable on a federal level, but they are exempt from state and local taxes.)

Taxable Debt Instruments

- **U.S. Treasury Bills**. When you buy a U.S. treasury bill, you are lending money to the U.S. government. U.S. treasury bills are the lowest risk investment available and are backed by the U.S. government. Treasury bills (T-bills) do not pay interest. They are purchased at a discounted rate, and at maturity they are worth the face value— much like a U.S. savings bond. The minimum purchase is $10,000 face value, and it will have a three-month, six-month, or one-year maturity. The T-bill is an excellent measuring stick to evaluate the risk versus return on other investments. This will be explained in greater depth later.

- **U.S. Treasury Notes**. Again, U.S. treasury notes are a loan to the U.S. government. A treasury note is an intermediate-term security with a two- to ten-year maturity. The minimum investment is $1,000, and notes pay interest semiannually. A note has a slightly higher risk than a bill because the term of investment is longer. Since the risk is higher, it should pay a higher rate of interest.

- **U.S. Treasury Bonds**. U.S. treasury bonds are a long-term investment or loan to the U.S. government. The maturities are ten years or longer. One thousand dollars is the minimum purchase. Treasury bonds pay the highest interest rate of all treasuries because long-term maturity increases risk of market fluctuations. The longer the term of investment, the higher interest rate the bond pays. Interest is paid semiannually. A thirty-year U.S. treasury bond is called the **long bond**. It is also used as a measuring stick to evaluate other investments.

Yield curves are often mentioned in relation to treasuries. The yield curve is the variation in returns between short-, intermediate-, and long-term investments. You should try to place your money where you will get the highest yield with the least amount of fluctuation.

- **Zero Coupon Bonds**. These will be discussed in greater detail later. Suffice it to say for now that they are instruments that are sold at a discounted amount, like treasury bills. They are highly susceptible to interest rate swings if sold before maturity. They are often used to fund college educations or retirement funds, because the purchaser can elect the actual date of maturity when she purchases the bond, and she knows the exact amount of the yield.

- **Government Agency Bonds**. Ginnie Mae, Fannie Mae, and Freddie Mac are the three most well known government agency bonds. These are bonds that are issued by mortgage associations and backed by government agencies but are not a direct obligation of the U.S. government. These are AAA rated. (Ratings are defined on page 43.)

- **Corporate Bonds**. When you buy corporate bonds, you lend money to a corporation.

These bonds are rated according to the creditworthiness of the issuer. The higher the credit rating of the corporation, the less interest paid to the bondholder. Corporate bonds are a perfect example of the risk versus reward relationship. The risk is directly proportional to the reward. The maturity can be short, intermediate, or long term. The longer the term, the higher the interest and the greater the risk. The minimum investment is $1,000.

Nontaxable Debt Instruments   The nontaxable instruments category is made up of one basic instrument—*municipal bonds*. Municipal bonds are sold by states, cities, or other local governments. They are traded in $5,000 increments. Maturities range from one month to forty years. Like corporate bonds, municipal bonds are also rated. They are exempt from federal taxes and can be exempt from state and local taxes providing you buy them from the state where you reside.

Interest Rates

Interest rates have been mentioned several times in this chapter because of their relationship to bonds. If interest rates go up, the value of bonds will go down. Or, if interest rates go down, the value of bonds goes up. (Refer to Figure 2.1.) If you have a bond paying 8 percent interest with a twenty-year maturity and interest rates fall to 6 percent, all the new bonds will be issued at 6 percent interest. Thus, investors would pay a pre-

Interest Rates   **Bond Values**

Interest Rates   **Bond Values**

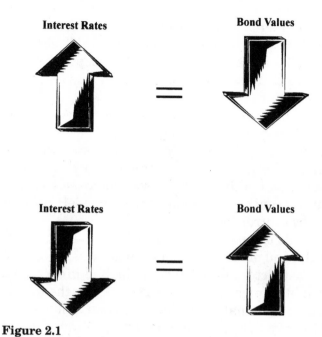

Figure 2.1

mium for the 8 percent instrument. For example, Mrs. Hill bought a ten-year treasury note for $1,000 at 8 percent interest. She collected interest semiannually for two years but then decided to cash in her bond before the maturity date. Her business had been a little slow, and she needed some extra capital. At the time she needed to sell her note, interest rates had risen to 9 percent, and she had to sell her 8 percent note for $900 instead of the $1,000 she paid for it.

In contrast, Mrs. Sullivan also bought a ten-year note for $1,000 at 8 percent interest. She held her note for five years, receiving interest semi-annually, until she also decided to sell her bond before the maturity date. Interest rates had dropped to 5 percent, so her 8 percent instrument was worth $1,300, $300 more than the $1,000 she paid for it. This is a very important concept. Take the time to understand it fully. Reread this section of the chapter if necessary.

If all of this information is new to you, it may seem rather overwhelming, but it will be worth the effort necessary to master these few concepts. Again, the goal is not to make you a financial analyst but rather to teach you the basics so that you can control your money instead of letting your money control you.

This is a lot of information for a new investor. At the end of the "Financial Awareness" program, the instructor admitted that she had presented a "weighty" program. However, she knew the importance of the material. She had been a housewife until six years ago, when her husband was injured in a car accident. He was in the hospital for several months, and his condition was critical for quite some time. She did not know what investments they had or what their financial picture looked like. Her husband is now fully recovered from his accident, but one thing did not return to the way it was before. She is now an informed partner. She went back to school to get a degree in finance and now has a voice in all of her family's financial matters. She wanted her friends to have that same sense of awareness that she now has and hoped that soon they would also be intrigued and excited by the markets.

In order to get excited, you have to know enough about investing to know how to make money. In the next chapter, you will start to learn how to make money with taxable bonds!

Let's summarize.

SUMMARY

- Three ways to make money on investments:
  1. By earning interest or dividends on the investment.
  2. By appreciation of the investment itself.
  3. Through a combination of the two known as **total return**.

- Investments are either equity (owner) or debt (loaner) investments.

- Owner investments are stocks, either common or preferred. When you buy stock, you are buying a piece of the company.

- Historically, stocks have proven to be the best investment.

- With a debt instrument investment, you are loaning your money to someone else, such as the U.S. government, a corporation, or a city, and they guarantee you a certain rate of return at the time of purchase and specify the time limit of the loan.

- Debt instruments can be either taxable or nontaxable.

- Taxable debt instruments are U.S. treasury bills, U.S. treasury notes, U.S. treasury bonds, zero coupon bonds, government agency bonds, and corporate bonds.

- Nontaxable debt instruments are municipal bonds.
- If interest rates go up, the value of bonds goes down. If interest rates go down, the value of bonds goes up.

UNDERSTANDING THE
TAXABLE BOND MARKET

"It is not the return on my investment that I am concerned about; it is the return of my investment."

— WILL ROGERS

You need an understanding of bonds and interest rates before investing in anything. Benjamin Graham, the "father of security analysis," taught his students to compare expected returns on companies to the predictable returns on AAA-rated utility bonds. He viewed utility bonds as providing risk-free returns for thirty years.

Warren Buffett, the second wealthiest man in the world in 1995, was a student of Graham's. Buffett improved upon his teacher's system in several ways. One of these was to compare the net cash flow of a company to the interest that could be earned on a thirty-year treasury bond.

George Soros, another giant among investors, also evaluates risk by comparing all interest rate risks to the return on the thirty-year bond. This method of analyzing risk versus reward has served him well over the years.

Successful investors intuitively understand a guaranteed cash flow and compare everything to the return on a U.S. treasury bond. One should weigh all investments against the treasury bond, but it is also a good idea to be even more cautious and to compare everything to the investment that is presumed to have the lowest risk—the treasury bill. No investment is without risk. Even the U.S. government could default on its loans.

This will be explained in greater depth as this book proceeds. In this chapter, you are going to begin to learn how to make money. Some of this information may seem like a review of material from Step II, but in the last chapter we were laying our foundation—now we will start building on it.

UNITED STATES TREASURIES

The most basic debt instruments are United States treasuries. U.S. treasuries are plain, straightforward, desirable instruments. They are infinitely easier for the unsophisticated investor to analyze than corporate or municipal debt. The market for U.S. debt instruments is the largest and most actively traded market in the world. It is an extremely liquid market. Liquidity is the ability of an instrument to be bought or sold quickly in various amounts without disturbing the price substantially. With treasuries, your money is readily available to you. You can sell treasuries, and the money, or principal and interest, must be in your account by the next day. The total of the U.S. debt outstanding is the federal deficit. The U.S. government's debt instruments are sold initially at an auction that is conducted once a week by the Federal Reserve. The actual amount of treasuries (or debt) for sale at the auction depends on the financing needs of the government. Another important point to remember is that no debt instruments have to be held to maturity. As mentioned earlier, U.S. treasuries are a good measuring stick for analyzing the risk versus reward of all other investments. If you can get a guaranteed return of 9 percent on a treasury bond, have your broker explain to you why you should accept the risk of buying a stock. This is important to consider before making any investment. Financial advisors often like to think of themselves as "stock guys," and some choose to ignore the bond market completely. Do not let this distorted view affect your investment career. We will look at several examples of this theory in action as we go along.

Many of you may be familiar with treasuries, but because of their importance as the foundation for our understanding of other investments, the following is a fact sheet listing the key characteristics of each.

Three Types of United States Treasuries

I. Treasury bills
   A. Do not pay interest—they are purchased at a discount and at maturity they are worth their face value.
   B. Minimum purchase is $10,000 face value.
   C. Have three-month, six-month, or one-year maturity.
   D. Are the lowest risk investment and are a good comparison for all other investments.

II. U.S. treasury notes
   A. Are intermediate-term securities.
   B. Have two- to ten-year maturity.
   C. Minimum investment is $1,000.
   D. Pay interest semiannually.
   E. Have higher risk than T-bills because term is longer.
   F. Generally pay 85 percent of the income that long-term bonds provide with less risk due to shorter maturity.

III. U.S. treasury bonds
   A. Are long-term investment (good comparison for all other investments).
   B. Maturities are ten years or longer.
   C. Minimum purchase is $1,000.
   D. Pay highest interest rate of all treasuries because longer term means more volatility.
   E. A thirty-year bond is called a *long bond*.

There are some basic facts that you need to know before developing a personal bond strategy. There are three strong forces that move the bond market. The first of these is the natural market force of supply and demand for money. For example, there is a limit to the amount (demand) the investor is willing to accept in interest for lending her money (supply) to the government.

The second strong force that moves the bond market is the Federal Reserve. The Federal Reserve raises or lowers interest rates to control the demand for money and thus controls the monetary environment. An investor must be cognizant of the "Fed" 's activity and what is going on with interest rates. Become a "Fed watcher"!

It is important to be aware of the two different market environments that also will affect your strategy. The first possibility is a positive market, or one in which interest rates are declining. The other possibility is a negative market, or one in which interest rates are rising. The direction of interest rates should be the first factor you consider before investing in anything!

The third force that moves the bond market is your fellow investors' perception of inflation—correct or incorrect. This will affect the real or actual return on bonds. If investors are putting a lot of money into the bond market, they are convinced that inflation will not erode their returns. Historically, you can expect to receive a return on your thirty-year treasury bond of about 3 percent above the inflation rate. If inflation is at 4 percent, you can expect the long bond to yield about 7 percent.

There are two common strategies that the investor needs to examine, but first be warned not to commit your money for a term longer than ten years. Every investor wants to make the most money for the least amount of risk, and history has proven that intermediate-term investments (with treasuries, that is two to ten years) have provided 85 percent of the income that long-term bonds provide with less risk due to the shorter maturity. Be aware that you can purchase in the open market an existing bond that may have been issued twenty-five years prior and still has five years remaining before maturity. This is interchangeable with a five-year note. The only reason for an individual to invest longer term, or up to thirty years, is to speculate on the direction of interest rates. The long bond is purchased frequently by those managing pension plans and speculators.

Keeping our ten-year rule in mind, let's look at laddered portfolios. This is an effective strategy that uses staggering maturities so that you have a treasury issue maturing every year for ten years. Every year, as one instrument matures, you would purchase another maturing in ten years. This is used to level out fluctuations in interest rates. It is used effectively with treasury, corporate, and municipal debt and is a simple strategy for an individual to implement in her own account.

The second strategy is actively managed portfolios for total return. This is a strategy that requires constant attention. It is recommended that it be left to the discretion of a professional manager. Your portfolio manager must constantly take the pulse of the markets. When a market starts to fluctuate, adjustments are made. For instance, if interest rates start to turn up and we are in a negative market, treasuries are sold and repurchased at shorter maturities to reduce the risk. When interest rates start to peak, you would want to extend maturities to capitalize on the higher return. This strategy is used to acquire both capital appreciation and to earn interest, that is, to reinvest. This is, by definition, total return. The key to this strategy is to remember that bills, notes, and bonds can be sold prior to maturity. The actively managed portfolios for total return strategy can be used most effectively with treasuries and corporates. Municipals are not as liquid. Be sure to be aware of the commission you are paying if you use this method. A flat fee is a better structure for the individual.

Make sure you understand the theory of buying and selling based on the interest rate environment, but do not be too concerned if you do not understand how to figure out if the current environment is positive or negative. There are many indicators that you should consider when forming your opinion on the current environment, but the single most important thing to consider is the monetary environment. There are some very knowledgeable people who publish this information. In fact, every major brokerage firm has economists who address this issue. An accurate and consistent source for this information is Bill Helman's Monetary Pressure Index, shown in Figure 3.1. (Bill Helman is the director of economics and investment policy for a major brokerage firm.) This chart is clear, simple to read, and a personal favorite of many informed investors. If the indicators are above 1, the environment is positive. If the indicators are below 1, the environment is negative. This chart can be used for determining

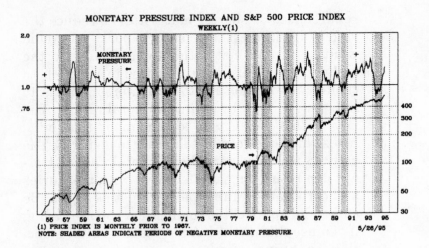

Figure 3.1   Helman's Monetary Pressure Index

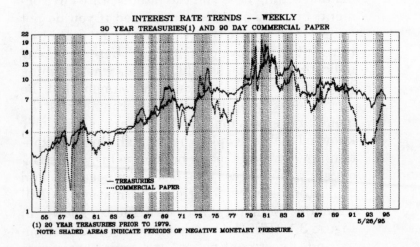

Figure 3.2   Interest Rate Trends

the market environment for both stocks and bonds. The shaded areas indicate periods of negative monetary pressure. Notice the relationships shown in Figure 3.1. When the Monetary Pressure Index is positive (above the 1.0 line), the Standard and Poor's 500 Index (S&P 500 Index) also goes up, or is positive. The S&P 500 Index is an average of 500 stocks that are listed on the New York Stock Exchange. Another interesting correlation exists between Figures 3.1 and 3.2. When the Monetary Pressure Index is positive (in the white area), the interest rates on the thirty-year treasury bonds are going down. When the interest rate or yield on a bond goes down, the price goes up, thus giving us a positive stock and bond market.

Investing is a very individualized undertaking. In order to personalize it for each of you, we have developed three sample composite women. Hopefully you will be able to identify with one of the three or at least to realize that you are a combination of two of them. We will look at investments through the criteria of the three composites, and then we will make recommendations for each (see Figure 3.3).

Terry Brooks is the first composite. She is thirty-three years old and was married for ten years to a medical student, who is now on the verge of a successful career. Terry has two children and has always worked outside the home. She is a fourth-grade teacher and earns $36,000 per year. A few months ago, Terry's husband informed her that he wanted a divorce. She is now facing the future as a single parent with little financial security. Her former husband pays child support and will pay for the children's college educations, but her own financial future is up to her. She wants to accumulate wealth.

Jean Cooper is next. She is fifty-five years old and is a successful Realtor making around $70,000 per year. Jean has been happily married for thirty

years to Bob, an advertising executive with a
prominent firm, and they have three children.
Bob's salary is $150,000 per year. Their oldest son
has graduated from college, but they still have one
daughter in college and another daughter who is a
senior in high school. Jean and Bob are both looking forward to retiring and having the time to
spend together and the money to travel when their
youngest child graduates from college. Bob is encouraging Jean to take more initiative in learning
about investments, and he would like for her to
handle their account, thus freeing up his already
hectic schedule. Jean is anxious to learn and has
set retirement planning as a top priority.

Lauren Sutton is the final composite. She is
seventy-two years old and has been a widow for
two years. Her husband was a very successful busi-
nessman, so Lauren never needed to work outside
the home. She raised four children and is very
active in volunteer work in her church and community. Lauren feels strongly the responsibility
that accompanies wealth. If she invested unwisely
and lost her money, she would not be able to
replace it. She wants the security of knowing that
she will not be a burden to her children in her later
life and would like to pass money on to her children and grandchildren upon her death. Until her
husband died, all Lauren knew of investing was
limited to certificates of deposit (CDs). These are
available at banks, savings and loans, and brokerage firms. She learned quickly that brokerage
firms often get you a better interest rate, because
they can shop many different banks for the best
rate. CDs have a maturity date, a guaranteed
interest rate, and a penalty for early withdrawal.

After her husband's death, Lauren learned of many other investments that were equally as safe as CDs and even more profitable. Now let's look at treasuries through the individual circumstances of our three women. Before we can make any specific recommendations, we must first determine the current market environment. For the purpose of our discussion, we will assume that it is positive. Given this information, we are ready to adopt a strategy for treasuries.

Let's start with Lauren. Lauren should be our largest investor in treasuries because she needs income, regardless of the market conditions. Thirty percent of her money should be invested in treasuries. In our positive environment with stable or declining interest rates, her maturities should range from two to ten years. Her strategy should be a combination of laddered portfolio (for income) and actively managed portfolio (for total return, capital appreciation, and interest). The more positive the monetary environment, the more her maturities should be weighted toward the ten-year range.

In a negative environment, she should shorten maturities to protect her principal. We would suggest two- to five-year maturities for income. Another good idea in a negative environment is to put money in a three-month or six-month treasury bill or a money market account in order to take advantage of the rising interest rates. One other effective course of action is to buy an issue trading at a premium. These issues are bought at a premium, or a percentage above the face value. The premium buys you a higher interest rate, or coupon. Many unsophisticated investors avoid these because they

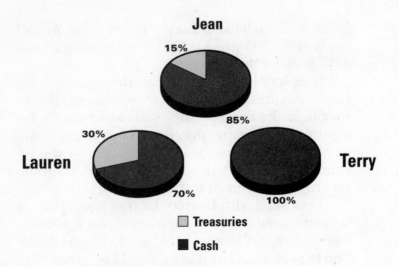

Figure 3.3   Positive Environment

dislike paying the additional premium, but in a negative environment, they are often cost effective because the higher coupon buffers the portfolio against rising interest rates. Be sure you compare the actual return of a premium instrument to the return on a par or discounted issue before you make your final decision.

Now let's look at a strategy for Jean, who is hoping to retire in five years. In our present positive environment, approximately 15 percent of her portfolio should be in treasuries, using the actively managed portfolio for total return strategy. Jean and Bob are making a comfortable living. They do not need income, but safety of principal becomes more of a factor the closer they get to retirement. The more positive the monetary environment, the more Jean's maturities should be extended toward the ten-year range. In a negative environment, they also should move into short-term treasury bills with three-month or six-month maturities or money market accounts.

Lastly, let's look at Terry's strategy. Treasuries are not for Terry. Her investment opportunities are coming up soon. We do not want the readers who identify with Terry to feel left out, so next we will examine a bond that might interest them—zero coupon bonds.

ZERO COUPON BONDS

Zero coupon bonds are sold at a discounted amount like treasury bills. The term of maturity is usually ten years or longer. Upon maturity, they pay the full face value. For example, if you buy a zero coupon bond for $500, at maturity it will pay $1,000. You receive no interest during the holding period. These bonds are backed by the U.S. government, but they are issued by brokerage firms, corporations, or municipalities. They are often used to fund a child's college education or for a retirement plan, because the purchaser can pick the actual date of maturity and know the exact amount she or he will make.

There are certain negative factors associated with zero coupon bonds. They have extremely volatile price swings and are highly susceptible to interest rate swings if sold before maturity. Another negative is that although no interest is actually paid until maturity, interest is taxed annually unless it is in an individual retirement account (IRA).

Terry should open an IRA, if she does not already have one. The maximum annual investment is $2,000. Terry should buy a zero coupon bond in her IRA for $1,000 if she can get a rate of 9 percent or higher. If the rate is below 9 percent, she is better off in stock. She should invest the other $1,000 in a more aggressive stock fund. That way, Terry is assured that her initial investment will be there when she is ready to retire, and it allows her to invest the other half of her money more aggressively. She will also avoid being taxed on the interest as long as the money remains in her IRA. In our current positive environment, stocks are a better value than zero coupon bonds, so Terry should wait and learn about investing in stocks.

GOVERNMENT AGENCY BONDS

Government agency bonds were formed to promote housing and farming, and they are rarely purchased by an individual. However, they may be part of a mutual fund portfolio. Government agency bonds should really be selected by a government agency bond specialist who is capable of analyzing them, for they can be rather complicated and confusing. They pay interest monthly instead of semiannually. Another characteristic is that in addition to a monthly interest check, the bondholder also receives a portion of the principal.

None of our women should invest in government agency bonds.

CORPORATE DEBT

Corporate debt is our last topic for this chapter. This is another area that most investors should avoid. Picking the "right" corporate debt instrument is a tricky business, for there are many variables affecting the price, so selections should be left to the experts. Another reason to avoid corporate debt is that the interest spread between corporate debt and treasuries is usually small and not worth the additional risk. However, to be fully educated on debt instruments, investors should know something about corporate debt.

Corporate debt consists of short-term corporate debt, notes, and bonds. When you buy a corporate instrument, you are lending money to a corporation. Commissions are often higher on corporate debt than on treasuries, so be an informed client.

Corporate debt, as well as municipal and government agency debt instruments, are all rated. U.S. treasuries are not rated, but they are the highest quality of all. The ratings of an instrument affect the price. Standard and Poor's and Moody's are rating services. Ratings can range anywhere from AAA through C. Government agency bonds have the highest ratings of AAA, and corporate debt can be rated anywhere on the scale. Its ratings depend on such factors as the creditworthiness of the corporation. Pension plans, municipal bond funds, and institutional investors usually do not purchase an instrument with a rating below BBB.

Both corporate and municipal debt instruments are affected by interest rate fluctuations. They both have a provision known as a **call feature**. This means that if interest rates go down, the issuer, most often a corporation or municipality, can redeem the instrument. The premium paid and when it is paid are predetermined.

Another variation of corporate debt is a "convertible." Again, this is not a recommendation for an individual to buy a convertible. Convertibles allow the investor to convert a corporate bond to corporate common stock. Convertibles have a maturity date, conversion price, coupon rate, ratings, and call dates. You would buy a convertible if you like the common stock but want a higher cash flow while you wait for the stock to appreciate. When the stock goes up, you can convert your bond to stock.

Let's review.

SUMMARY

- There are three types of U.S. treasury instruments—bills, notes, and bonds.
- Use the thirty-year treasury bond as a measuring stick to evaluate all other investments.
- We recommend that you also use the six-month T-bill rate when evaluating other investments.

- There are two commonly used bond strategies—laddered portfolios and actively managed portfolios for total return.
- Intermediate-term investments have provided 85 percent of the income that long bonds have provided, with less risk.
- Zero coupon bonds are sold at a discount; government backed but issued by brokerage firms, corporations, or municipalities; often used to fund college educations or retirement plans because the purchaser can pick date of maturity; susceptible to volatile price swings if sold before maturity.
- U.S. treasuries are simple instruments and are preferred over corporate debt and government agency bonds.
- Be sure to determine the monetary environment before you invest in anything.

When you feel comfortable with this information, we will continue with municipal bonds or non-taxable instruments.

Step IV

Demanding Quality in Tax-Free Instruments

"Every gold coin you earn is a golden slave that can work for you."

—*George S. Clason*

The possibility of default on municipal bonds by Orange County, California, is a reminder that it is imperative to pay more for the quality found in AAA-rated, insured, or prerefunded bonds. A broker had placed one of his largest clients with a money manager who specialized in California municipal bonds. His client needed tax-free income and was often unavailable when decisions needed to be made, so the portfolio manager had the authority to move in and out of bonds at will. A bond manager is *supposed* to have the expertise to select bonds other than AAA-rated, insured, or prerefunded bonds, but this is not always the case, and it certainly is not a task for an individual with little or no prior experience.

This broker had been alerted to a possible problem with the Orange County bonds a few days prior to the trouble and had voiced his concern to the bond manager, who assured him that everything was fine—there was absolutely no danger. When it became known that Orange County had mismanaged its finances and was now facing bankruptcy, the broker's client's AA-rated bond dropped to a C rating. When a bond's rating is dropped or raised, it dramatically affects the price of the bond. In this case, fear took hold of the entire bond market.

This situation triggered a series of events. The broker called in his branch manager, who in turn called the firm's regional president, who called in the head of his firm's municipal research department in order to protect the client's interests. When the concerned broker was reassured that his client was in no danger of losing his investment, the broker got on the phone and fired the bond manager for not following the client's investment parameters. This was not the first time that the manager had put him in an uncomfortable situation. The manager's opinion on the direction of interest rates was in direct conflict with the broker, who had instructed the manager to employ a total return strategy, not a buy and hold management style. The manager's ego got in the way, and he did not want to admit that he had made a mistake. The broker refused to let his client suffer because the manager could not follow directions.

The reason an investor goes to a full-service brokerage firm is to receive service and guidance. This was an example of all of the firm's employees pulling together to protect the client. However, investors should know that no investment is completely without risk. The best way to protect yourself is to know everything you can about every investment you consider.

Let's begin the discussion with general information about municipal debt. It is sold by states, cities, or other local governments, generally for the purpose of financing the building of roads, schools, bridges, or hospitals. Municipal debt can be either short-term notes, intermediate-term notes, or bonds. It is usually sold in $5,000 increments, and maturities range from one month to forty years. All of these debt instruments are rated, and all are exempt from federal taxes. They can be exempt from state and local taxes if you purchase the issue from the state and municipality in which you reside.

Brokers are paid commissions on all types of bonds, including corporate bonds, treasuries, and municipals. The commission rates vary. You should always ask your broker the commission rate that is actually being charged, because it is included in the price of the bond. This is an area where the client has to be aware, because an unethical broker can hide costly commissions in a bond's purchase price. Shorter maturity bonds should have less commissions on the purchase side, and, if they are sold before maturity, the commission should be even lower. The purchaser should make sure that she is informed.

Since municipal bond interest is exempt from federal tax, the amount of interest, or yield, will be lower than that from treasury or corporate debt of equal maturity. You should always consider the after-tax yield, or the actual amount of income you keep after taxes are deducted. Let's look at an example. Lauren is trying to decide how to invest $10,000. A ten-year U.S. treasury bond is paying 8 percent interest, or $800 per year. However, Lauren is in a 36 percent tax bracket, so she will get to keep only $512 of the interest earned because $288 is paid in taxes. If she purchases $10,000 of municipal bonds from the state and municipality in which she resides with the same ten-year maturity and a 6 percent interest rate, she will actually keep the entire $600 per year that is earned, for there will be no taxes on this money. After analyzing the two, it becomes clear that the municipal bond will actually give her a higher return.

There is one other point to consider. If interest rates drop and Lauren decides to sell her 6 percent bond in five years for $12,000 instead of the $10,000 that she paid for it, she will owe capital gains tax on the $2,000 profit on the bond. The interest that she has earned during the holding period is always tax exempt.

The two most common types of municipal bonds are general obligation bonds and revenue bonds. General obligation bonds (GOs) comprise 35 percent of the municipal bond market. They are backed by the full faith and taxing power of the issuer, or, in other words, the issuer will raise taxes without limit to repay you. These are considered to be more secure than revenue bonds, so they will pay a lower interest rate than other municipal bonds.

Revenue bonds are backed by a specific revenue source instead of the full taxing power of the municipality. For example, to build a new hospital, revenue bonds could be sold. The revenues of the hospital will pay back the principal and interest of the bonds. In the case of default, the hospital (the asset itself) backs the bond. These bonds are less secure than general obligation bonds and so pay a higher interest rate. Revenue bonds comprise 50 percent of all municipal issues. The remaining 15 percent of municipal bonds sold are special types of bonds such as special tax bonds, special assessment bonds, moral obligation bonds, double-barrel bonds, and industrial development bonds. For our purposes, these need not be discussed.

Another type of municipal debt that merits discussion is the short-term municipal note. These instruments have a maturity ranging from three months to three years. They are issued to raise money for temporary financing of capital improvements or to even out cash flows of municipalities. These notes could very well fit into an individual's portfolio.

There are companies that insure municipal debt. These companies analyze the municipal debt based on ratings and soundness, and then they provide the municipality with insurance for both the principal and interest of the debt. The municipality actually pays the premium, but insured issues typically pay about 0.5 percent less than similar uninsured issues, therefore passing along the cost to the purchaser.

There are seven companies that offer this particular type of insurance:

1. American Municipal Bond Assurance Corporation (AMBAC)

2. Municipal Bond Insurance Association Corporation (MBIAC)

3. Financial Guaranty Insurance Corporation (FGIC)

4. Bond Investors' Guaranty Insurance Corporation (BIGI)

5. Financial Security Assurance Corporation (FSA)

6. Capital Markets Assurance Corporation (CAPMAC)

7. Capital Guaranty Insurance Company (CGIC)

We recommend that you buy only AAA-rated, insured issues or prerefunded bonds. A prerefunded bond is callable, but at some time before the call date arrives, the municipality backs the bond with U.S. treasuries. A city or municipality has a limit to the amount of debt it can have on its books. When a municipality prerefunds a bond, this removes the bond from the books and enables the municipality to sell more bonds. When determining whether or not to purchase a prerefunded bond, the purchaser should check the return at the designated call date, rather than at the maturity date, to see if it is a lucrative investment. When a bond is prerefunded, the call date becomes the

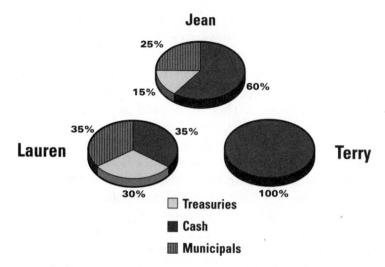

Figure 4.1   Positive Environment

maturity date and the rating becomes AAA. These bonds trade at lower yields but are the safest form of municipal investing.

Again, let's look at individual investment advice for our three composite women (see Figure 4.1). Let's begin with Terry. She should not have any municipal debt instruments, but she still needs a working knowledge of them. There are many other investment possibilities for Terry that would better serve her needs.

Jean is next. In her situation of planning for retirement, she should have 25 percent of her money in municipal debt using a laddered strategy. This brings her total investment exposure to 40 percent.

Lauren should have 35 percent of her money invested in municipal debt in order to provide income. Her strategy is a laddered approach. Lauren's total bond exposure is now 65 percent. Most high net worth individuals own conservative debt instruments. In a positive environment, bonds and notes will outperform money markets or cash equivalents, so they are a good place to be. In a negative environment, bond maturities should be shortened, or the client should have a greater percentage of her money in treasury bills, short-term municipal notes, and money markets. Safety of principal is your first concern in a negative environment. The market will eventually provide you with a chance to take advantage of the higher yields offered in longer term securities.

Let's summarize.

SUMMARY

- Municipal debt is sold by states, cities, or other local governments, usually to finance the building of roads, schools, bridges, and hospitals.

- Municipal debt can be short-term notes, intermediate-term notes, or longer term bonds with maturities ranging from one month to forty years.

- Municipal debt is usually sold in $5,000 increments.

- Municipal debt is exempt from federal taxes and can be exempt from state and local taxes if you purchase the issue from the state and municipality in which you reside.

- Commissions are included in the price of a bond, so know what you are paying when you are buying or selling.

- The two most common types of municipal bonds are general obligation bonds (GOs) and revenue bonds. General obligation bonds are backed by the full faith and taxing power of the issuer and are more secure than revenue bonds. Revenue bonds are backed by a specific revenue source instead of the full taxing power of the municipality; for example, a hospital will back its own hospital revenue bond.

- Short-term municipal debt instruments have maturities ranging from three months to three years and could fit very nicely into an individual's portfolio.

- There are seven companies that insure municipal debt based on soundness and ratings. Most people should only buy AAA-rated, insured issues, or prerefunded bonds.

- A prerefunded bond is backed by U.S. treasuries before its call date arrives so that the municipality can remove it from its books and sell more bonds. When a bond is prerefunded, the call date becomes the maturity date, the rating becomes AAA, and they trade at lower yields.

In the next chapter, we will begin to really get into the information that most of you have been waiting for. We are going to begin to learn about stocks.

SIMPLIFYING THE LANGUAGE OF COMMON STOCK

". . . there are no good stocks—they are all bad . . . unless they go up."
—WILLIAM J. O'NEIL

Keep in mind your purpose for learning this information. It might be a little different for each person, but it can be capsulized into one idea: *security through financial independence.* To achieve this goal, you must lay certain building blocks. It would be much more fun to just pick successful stocks, but you must first know what categories of stocks are available and then when to select each one. It is also important to know who should buy stocks. The stock market is not for everyone. If a person has the extra income or cash after the essentials—the house, health insurance, auto and life insurance—have been taken care of, then the stock market is a possibility. Bear with us on the slow, informative parts of this chapter, and you will soon have the tools to pick winning stocks responsibly. Investing is not based on luck.

Stocks are equity or owner instruments. They are called equity or owner instruments because the purchaser is actually buying a piece of a company. A good starting point is often an employee stock option program at your place of employment. This is one of the simplest and most effective methods of accumulating wealth. You can often purchase the stock at a discount and with "before-tax" dollars. There is also a special sense of satisfaction in owning stock in the company where you work. Check with your company's benefits department for available options.

With that purchase, as with any purchase, there should be pride of ownership. You should own shares of stock in companies that you like and want to hold for a long time. This is not to say that you should not ever trade or sell your stock, just that there are two schools of thought. The first is a buy and hold philosophy, and the second philosophy is concerned with asset allocation between stocks, bonds, and cash. A combination of these two philosophies is the most effective if you can competently do it. Historically, looking back to 1926, stocks have proven to be the best asset class to own. The expected return from being fully invested in stocks is around 10 percent—approximately 4 percent of that comes from dividends and 6 percent comes from price appreciation. However, if you look at recent returns, you will see that the

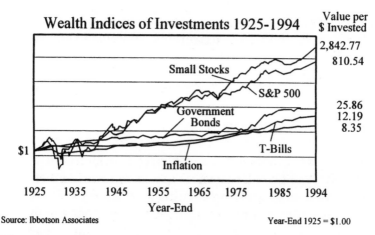

Figure 5.1   Ibbotson Chart

market has not met that expectation. The return for the one-year period ending December 31, 1994, was only 1.32 percent, for the three-year period the return was 6.27 percent, and over five years it averaged 8.70 percent. The Ibbotson chart (Figure 5.1) illustrates this point. An Ibbotson chart plots the historic return on treasury bills, treasury bonds, large-cap stocks found in the S&P 500, small-cap stocks, and inflation. It generally goes back to 1926. Conventional wisdom is that small-cap stocks are the most volatile but by far the preferred asset class for appreciation and return. Our personal research does not bear this out. Measured by the Value Line Index from December 1975 to March 1995, small-cap stocks have underperformed the large-cap S&P 500 companies. We recommend that you buy large-cap stocks in solid companies. You minimize your risk, and you could actually increase your returns. You will understand this better as we move through our explanation of the different types of stocks. We are not disregarding smaller companies, but we are going to show you how to be extremely selective in choosing them.

GROWTH STOCKS

There are four basic categories of common stock. The first is growth stock. A growth stock is stock with a steadily growing earning stream, regardless of the economic environment. Growth stocks also have a higher price-to-earnings ratio. The price-to-earnings ratio is the ratio that is derived from dividing the price of the stock by the annual earnings per share. Growth stocks work well in a buy and hold philosophy, because they generally do well in the long term.

A broker, Ben, was looking for stocks for his children in the early 1980s. He came upon a company called Berkshire Hathaway (BRK on the New York Stock Exchange). This is an insurance company run by Warren Buffett and used primarily as a holding company to make other investments. It is a prime example of a growth stock. According to the November 11, 1994, *Value Line*, Buffett never invests in a business until he fully understands its dynamics and respects the operating management. He then buys and holds—regardless of the performance. His philosophy has produced an enviable long-term track record. Berkshire Hathaway was trading at $500 per share in the early 1980s. Ben purchased ten shares for each child. Today, in 1995, the same stock is trading at $32,500 per share.

Large-Cap Growth Stocks

There are three broad classifications of growth stocks. Large-capitalization growth stocks are the first classification. These are commonly called large-cap growth stocks. Capitalization is the price of the stock times the amount of shares outstanding. Stocks of large, mature, well-known companies are called large-cap growth stocks. Examples are companies such as Gillette, Disney, and Coca-Cola. These stocks have moderate risk but are thought to have moderate returns. However, high-quality stocks can have periods where they outperform those of the smaller, more volatile companies. Growth of large-cap growth stocks is steady in all economic cycles. They normally reinvest the profits or earnings of the company instead of paying a high dividend. If they successfully invest, it results in a high percentage of return on your equity. In other words, you are making money on your investment, and eventually, the price of the stock should go up. These can be referred to as "blue chips."

Mid-Cap Growth Stocks

Next let's examine mid-cap growth stocks. These are stocks from medium-sized companies. There is slightly more risk with mid-cap growth stocks than with large-cap growth stocks, but there is also the possibility of higher returns. Examples of mid-cap growth stocks are The Limited, Pier One Imports, and Reebok.

Small-Cap Growth Stocks

Finally, there are small-cap growth stocks. These are the youngest, fastest growing companies. They offer the highest risk but also the possibility of the highest returns. These stocks can be very volatile. Two good examples of small-cap growth stocks are Fastenal and CUC International.

CYCLICAL STOCKS

Before you can possibly know which stock to buy and when, you must first understand the different types of stocks. The second category of common stocks is cyclical stocks. Cyclical stocks are sensitive to economic cycles. The earnings per share can vary based on the strength or weakness in the economy. This makes the earnings of cyclical stocks more volatile. This will be clearer as examples are given. Cyclical stocks may pay higher quarterly dividends to the stockholders instead of reinvesting the profits into the company. There are three types of cyclical stocks: large-cap cyclical, mid-cap cyclical, and small-cap cyclical.

Large-Cap Cyclical Stocks

Large-cap cyclicals are stocks from big, mature companies. They offer the stockholder moderate risk but also moderate return. Large-cap cyclical stocks have a lower price-to-earnings ratio than mid-cap and small-cap cyclicals. Large-cap cyclical stocks can be "blue chip" stocks. A perfect example of a large-cap cyclical stock is General Motors. During a recession, people cannot afford to purchase new cars, so the earnings drop considerably. However, as economic conditions improve, all of the people who have been postponing a car purchase decide that it is time to buy the car. Possibly they are tired of spending money on their old car and conclude that it is more cost effective for the long term, or perhaps they are just feeling better and more secure about their personal situation and the economy in general. Regardless, they buy the car. High volumes of car sales cause General Motors' earnings to rise considerably.

After the 1987 stock market crash, General Motors' price per share dropped significantly, causing the actual dividend yield to jump to 9 percent. If you purchase a share of stock for $100 that is paying a 5 percent (or $5) annual dividend and the price per share drops to $50 per share, the annual $5 dividend now becomes 10 percent. People often purchase a stock solely for the dividend or income. In this example, General Motors was paying a higher interest rate than one could get on bonds, plus there also was the possibility of the price appreciation on the stock itself. It was like getting paid while you waited for your stock to go up.

Mid-Cap Cyclical Stocks

Mid-cap cyclicals are stocks of moderate-sized companies. They have a higher risk but also a higher return than large-cap cyclical stocks. An example of a mid-cap cyclical is the Ryland Group, a home-building company that is thus extremely sensitive to interest rate fluctuations.

Small-Cap Cyclical Stocks

Small-cap cyclical stocks are stocks from smaller companies. They provide the highest risk but can also provide a high return. A good example of a small-cap cyclical stock is Sterling Electronics.

DEFENSIVE STOCKS

The third category of stocks with which you need to be familiar is defensive stocks. Defensive stocks are stocks that do well in a slow economic environment. Examples of defensive stocks are food stocks, soaps, and utilities. These are stocks from companies producing products that people are still going to need even in a recession. Utility stocks grow their dividends slowly. They offer a high yield and are usually purchased for the dividend. Utility stocks are an early indicator of the direction of the overall markets and interest rates. The Dow Jones Utility Average is an index of utility stocks. These stocks are also interest rate sensitive. If interest rates are heading down, utilities tend to turn up. When interest rates are heading up, utilities turn down. The Dow Jones Utility Average can be one of the best leading indicators of the upcoming direction of the stock market. The Dow Jones Utility Average usually points the way for the Dow Jones Industrial Average. Although this is not an ironclad rule, its percentage of accuracy is high.

Utilities are perceived to be a conservative investment. However, in November 1992, one particular broker recommended that his clients sell their utilities and reinvest the money in another area. Utilities went on to lose 30 to 35 percent of their value. This is a large loss and not in the least conservative. The broker did not repurchase utilities for his clients until December 1994. Examples of utility stocks are *Kansas City Power and Light* and *Southern Company*.

AMERICAN DEPOSITORY RECEIPTS

American depository receipts (ADRs) comprise our final category of common stock. These are certificates that represent ownership of foreign shares that are held abroad by U.S. banks located in a foreign country. ADRs are subject to currency fluctuations and can be either growth or cyclical. The investor in an ADR receives both the dividend and capital appreciation in U.S. dollars. Two excellent examples of ADRs are Sony and Toyota.

Non-U.S. investments are the fastest growing area in investments. Exposure almost doubled in the last twenty-five years. It is an excellent way for investors to increase their return and reduce their risk.

VALUE INVESTING

There are three terms that require further explanation, because they will come up in discussions from time to time: value investing, blue chips, and top-down approach. First let's look at value investing. We find the entire theory absurd because it is based on the concept of attempting to buy low and sell higher, and all investing should be value investing from this standpoint. With value investing, you are investing in companies that are perceived to be unloved or out of favor. The concept is based upon the theory that the market is inefficient and does not truly reflect the actual or intrinsic value of a company. The current price per share is perceived to be low compared to the company's historic price-to-earnings ratios, cash flows, book value, or dividends.

Three typical examples of stocks fall into this category. The first of these is *turnarounds*. A turnaround is a company that is restructuring debt, restructuring management, or restructuring debt and management.

Asset plays are the next example of value investing. Asset plays involve undervalued assets on the books of a corporation. Examples of these might be oil and gas, real estate that the corporation has been holding for many years, or overfunded pension plans. The idea is to take advantage of these undervalued items and buy low.

A third example of value investing is a *special situation*, usually associated with a takeover candidate. In a special situation, you are buying for a specific, expected result and fundamental change.

The characteristics may not be easily recognizable to the majority. An asset play can be a special situation if it is purchased for a specific, expected result and fundamental change.

BLUE CHIP STOCKS

The second term to be discussed is blue chip stocks. These can be growth or cyclical. These are often perceived to be the least risky. They are stocks from the biggest companies. The thirty Dow Jones Industrial stocks are in this category. Exercise caution when you hear the term "blue chip." Do not feel a false sense of security about owning blue chip stocks. A blue chip can go down in value—it is not a guarantee of safety. Do not limit yourself to any one category of stocks, but rather stay flexible.

TOP-DOWN APPROACH

The third and final term to understand is top-down approach. Understanding a top-down approach will prepare you for our next discussion on how to pick individual stocks. This is our preferred approach for buying and selling stocks. With this method, you first examine the economy to find out where it is. There are four stages: recession, early stage recovery, late stage recovery, and expansion. If there is a recession, there is high unemployment, weak demand for goods, and a turning down of services and interest rates.

In an early stage recovery, interest rates fall further, the demand for goods and services starts to pick up, and employment starts to rise.

A late stage recovery is characterized by interest rates beginning to stabilize and demand for goods and services strengthening further.

The expansion stage exists when interest rates are rising, employment is strong, there is a high demand for goods and services, prices increase, and there is overall inflation.

After you have examined the economy, then you should determine which group of stocks to own.

In a recession, you want to own necessities such as the food and beverage group, soaps, utilities, and cosmetics.

In an early stage recovery, you want to own consumer cyclicals such as housing, automobiles, retailers, and lodging.

During a late stage recovery, you want to own raw materials, paper, chemicals, energy, metals, and technology.

In an expansion period, you want to own capital goods such as steels, machinery, and electrical/industrial.

It may seem difficult for you to determine the current economic stage, but after we have discussed technical analysis, you will understand how to determine trends in certain stock groups.

Let's summarize.

SUMMARY

- Stocks are owner or equity instruments.

- Stocks have proven to be the best asset class to own with the expected return from being fully invested at around 10 percent.

- There are four basic categories of stock: growth stock, cyclical stock, defensive stock, and American depository receipts (ADRs).

- There are three kinds of growth stocks: large-cap, mid-cap, and small-cap.

- Capitalization is the price of the stock times the number of shares outstanding.

- Large-cap growth stocks are stocks of large, mature companies. They have moderate risk and often have moderate returns, but growth is steady in all economic cycles. They normally reinvest the profits or earnings of the company instead of paying a high dividend. Examples are Gillette, Coca-Cola, and Disney.

- Mid-cap growth stocks are stocks of medium-sized companies with slightly more risk than large-cap growth companies, but there is also the possibility of higher returns. Examples are The Limited and Pier One Imports.

- Small-cap growth stocks are stocks from the youngest, fastest growing companies. They offer the highest risk and can be volatile but also provide the possibility of the highest returns. Examples are Fastenal and CUC International.

- Large-cap cyclical stocks are stocks from big, mature companies that are sensitive to the economic cycles. They generally pay higher quarterly dividends to the stockholders instead of reinvesting the profits into the company. They offer moderate risk and moderate return. General Motors is a good example of a large-cap cyclical.

- Mid-cap cyclicals are stocks of moderate-sized companies that have a higher risk and higher return potential than large-cap cyclicals. The Ryland Group is an example.

- Small-cap cyclicals are stocks from smaller companies that provide the highest risk and the highest return. Sterling Electronics is a good example of a small-cap cyclical.

- Defensive stocks are stocks that do well in a slow economic environment. Utility stocks are an example of defensive stocks. Utilities offer a high yield and are generally purchased for the dividend. Other examples of defensive stocks are food stocks and soaps.

- American depository receipts are certificates that represent ownership of foreign shares that are held abroad by U.S. banks located in a foreign country. They are subject to currency fluctuations and can be either growth or cyclical. Both the dividend and capital appreciation are paid in U.S. dollars. Sony and Toyota are examples.

- Value investing is investing in companies that are perceived to be unloved and out of favor so that you can buy low and sell higher. The following are three examples of value investing: *turnarounds* are companies that are restructuring debt or management or both; *asset plays* involve undervalued assets on the books of a corporation such as oil and gas, or real estate that it has been holding for many years, or overfunded pension plans that you can take advantage of by buying low; and *special situations* involve buying for a specific purpose for a specific, expected result and fundamental change, such as a takeover. Value investing can involve either growth or cyclical stocks.

- Blue chip stocks can be growth or cyclical. They are the biggest companies such as the thirty Dow Jones Industrial stocks, but they can go down in value and are not without risk.

- A top-down approach for buying and selling stocks involves deciding on the current economic stage—either a recession, early stage recovery, late stage recovery, or expansion—and then determining which groups of stocks to own based on the current economic stage.

Take some time to digest this information, but do not be overly concerned about identifying the

current economic cycle. Future discussions on
technical analysis will help clarify which groups
of stocks are likely to outperform.

The next chapter explains what most people
are eager to learn—how to pick individual stocks
and which stocks to own.

PICKING STOCKS— THE LOST ART

"Never invest in any idea you can't illustrate with a crayon."

—*PETER LYNCH*

You should make your stock decisions by using a top-down approach. First, you must decide whether to be in or out of the market and to what extent you want to be in or out. There are three things to consider before making this determination: interest rates, market psychology, and valuations.

You should examine interest rates first, because 80 percent of the decision will hinge on this. They determine the monetary environment and are the pulse of the market. If interest rates are falling, it is a positive environment for stocks. More money will flow into the stock market if money markets, bills, notes, and bonds are paying a lower interest rate. This will make stocks more desirable and thus increase demand for them.

Determining the monetary environment should not be a terribly difficult task for you at this point since you are now aware of the forces or dynamics in the U.S. treasury market. Think back to what we have learned about interest rates and their effect on the supply and demand for U.S. treasuries. This knowledge will now be valuable in understanding stock market principles. Remember, everyone is looking for the same result— getting the highest return with the lowest amount of risk. All people fear that the stock or bond market will turn down immediately after they commit their money. Trends in interest rates and stock market direction generally last for extended periods of time. By understanding the monetary environment, you reduce the risk of losing money and will have more confidence in your decisions. The direction of interest rates will dictate the flow of money into or out of all of the financial markets— money markets, bills, notes, bonds, and stocks. Look at the chart that Bill Helman created to illustrate this point. He refers to it as the Monetary Pressure Index (Figure 6.1). When it is positive, the stock market generally heads up. In Figure 6.1, dated December 15, 1994, it is still negative but is about to turn up just as the stock market makes a major advance. When it is negative (below 1.0), the market turns down. This type of information can be obtained from an informed broker at any major brokerage firm. If it is not this exact chart, it will include similar information. You do not need to be an economist to gather this data on your own. On

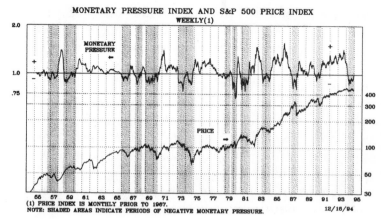

Figure 6.1 Monetary Pressure Index

Wall Street, you do not have to have all of the answers; you just have to know who does.

Secondly, you should investigate market psychology. To examine market psychology, you must first understand the concept. A poll of professional investment advisors is taken to determine their opinion on the direction of the market, be it bullish (a positive outlook for the market), bearish (a negative outlook for the market), or neutral. This consensus of investment advisors is most useful when it is tilted to an extreme. It is published daily in *Investor's Business Daily* with the title Psychological Market Indicators and can be found in the Markets Charts section. If the consensus becomes 50 to 60 percent bullish, it is probably time to be cautious about the overall market. If the report is 50 to 60 percent bearish, it is probably time to buy. If larger investors such as mutual funds and investment advisors are bearish, they most likely are holding a high percentage of their assets in cash or cash equivalents. Cash creates a pent-up demand for stock. If you buy at this point, prior to the larger investors, it is possible to ride the entire upturn if you select the right stock. The reason for this is that the majority of investors are generally wrong. When an opinion becomes too firmly entrenched, it is approaching a turning point. The opinion of professional investors should be viewed with skepticism. This can work to your advantage if you are willing to rely on yourself and formulate your own opinions.

The third element to consider is valuations. Valuations determine whether the market is historically high or low. It is necessary to understand valuations in order to determine the overall risk involved in the market. Remember, even good stocks can go down in a bad market. The market is viewed in relation to price-to-dividend ratios, price-to-earnings ratios, and price-to-book values.

Price-to-dividend ratios: If the dividend yields on the S&P 500 are below 3 percent, the market is overvalued from an historical level. You should use caution if purchasing. If it is above 4 percent, the market is undervalued, and it may be a buying opportunity. Ask your broker for this information. Keep in mind that the expected 10 percent return on stock investments is composed of 6 percent price appreciation and 4 percent dividends; therefore, a low dividend yield means you must get a higher price appreciation from the stock in order to achieve the 10 percent historic return. Do not be confused by some books and magazines that tell you to expect an easy 15 percent return; it probably will not happen, and it most certainly will not be easy.

Price-to-earnings ratios: If price-to-earnings ratios are high, in the upper teens or above, then the market is overvalued in relation to earnings. Again, use caution. A price-to-earnings ratio of ten or below is an indication of an undervalued market.

Price-to-book value: Price-to-book value is the third measurement of valuation, but it is becoming an outmoded method of measurement. Book value is the assumed valuation of a company if it were to be liquidated—all assets minus all liabilities. Lack of continuity in the valuation of assets makes it an ineffective tool. The Dow Jones valuations can also be found in the *Investor's Business Daily* on the same page as the bearish and bullish consensus. You can use these valuations as a gauge for extremes in the market. If you notice any extreme valuations in the Dow Jones Industrial Average, ask your broker for the same information on the S&P 500 Index. The S&P 500 Index is an index of 500 stocks, as opposed to the thirty issues that the Dow Jones Industrial Average considers. The S&P 500 is the classic index used when measuring valuations.

Remember that all three factors—valuations, interest rates, and market psychology—are rarely going to fall into place at the same time. Use the monetary environment (or the direction of interest rates) as the most heavily weighted indicator. Markets will not reverse trend merely because of over- or undervaluation. They can stay overvalued for prolonged periods of time, but they cannot withstand high valuations and rising interest rates occurring simultaneously. A negative monetary environment (or a time when interest rates

are rising) in combination with overvaluations can
cause the market to go down.

Once you have decided to get in the market, it
is necessary to look at the industry groups (such as
utilities, lodging, or automobile stock groups) to
decide which are showing technical strength.
Groups of stocks will show trends, and you are trying to identify them. You are better off owning a
weak stock in a strong group than a strong stock in
a weak group. We will be discussing technical
analysis in depth soon. One way to find out which
groups are strong is to ask your broker, who has
this information readily available through his or
her technical research department. If you want to
determine it on your own, look at the S&P industry
groups and charts located in the front of the Mansfield Charts (Figure 6.2). We will discuss the Mansfield Charts further later.

For the purpose of our discussion, let's say that
consumer cyclicals such as housing, automobiles,
and retailing are showing technical strength, even
though the newspapers and the news programs are
telling you that we are in a recession. This is happening because the market anticipates cycles before they occur, often by as much as six months. A
good example to explain this concept is the fashion industry. When you go to your local store to buy
your summer wardrobe, you buy what you think
are the latest styles, but actually, by the time those
fashions have arrived in your local stores, the fashion designers are designing styles that make your
things dated. Likewise, by the time the majority
of the people have realized we are in a recession
and pulled out of the market, the smart money has
jumped back in and purchased stocks that do well

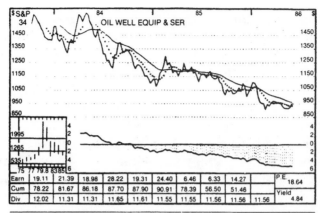

$S&P		84		85						86 $

SOURCE: Mansfield Stock Chart Service.

Figure 6.2   Mansfield Chart (Courtesy of Alan Shaw)

in an early stage recovery (such as housing, automobiles, retailers, and lodging) based on their
analysis of industry groups. The concept you need
to understand here is to try to focus on what is
going to happen rather than on what is occurring
at the present time. Often by the time information
filters down to the small investor, the money has
already been made or lost. By the same token, once
a "tip" appears in a magazine or newspaper, it is
already old news. Use this information as a gauge
for what everyone else knows and try to look
beyond it.

Now that we have examined industry groups
and determined which groups are showing
strength, we need to look at individual stocks that
are showing strength in our predetermined groups.
We will examine all stocks from two angles—technical analysis and fundamental analysis.

Always look at technical analysis first. Do not
even consider buying a stock without looking at

the technical patterns. Do not let the word "technical" frighten you. Technical analysis is actually quite simple. It is a chart of a stock's performance based on supply and demand. What actually makes stock go up or down is supply and demand. If a stock goes up today, that simply means more people wanted to buy than sell. This is what technical analysis charts. It is the picture of where the stock is in the supply and demand cycle. With technical analysis, one uses the price of a stock, the volume of trading and a certain time period to determine the direction of the stock's future price movement. Using technical analysis will give you an edge over many people on Wall Street because not all market participants use it. The majority of the research available is fundamental, and it is extremely biased toward the "buy" side. Some investors consider only the fundamentals of a company (see page 89). It is a definite advantage to analyze a company using both technical and fundamental analysis. If the technical patterns look good and the fundamental analysis is also strong, this reinforces your position. Look at the technicals first, because they will often indicate an emerging strength *before* it is reflected in the fundamentals. This never ceases to amaze us, and we have seen it happen time and again. The fact that everyone does not consult charts before selecting a stock makes no difference. We are teaching you the way we pick stocks, and it works for us. If you follow this direction, it can also work for you. Technical analysis is an art form. It is visual and fun to do!

There are predictable patterns that are clearly discernable. These can be either bullish or bearish.

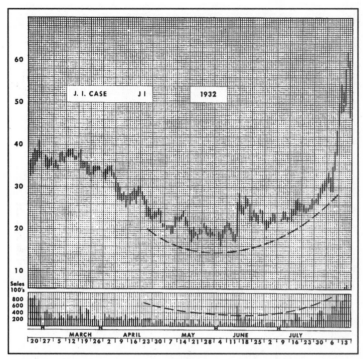

Figure 6.3   Saucer Bottom Pattern

Some of the bullish patterns are saucer bottom (Figure 6.3), double bottom (Figure 6.4), and head and shoulders bottom (Figure 6.5).

The resistance is the selling pressure or the overhead supply. Support is what happens when buyers come in and keep the price of the stock from falling lower. Breakout occurs when the stock has broken through the resistance and moves higher.

A saucer bottom is a favorite pattern. When this occurs, most of the sellers are out and demand has started back up. It is a relatively low-risk investment. The longer the period of time that a base is established, the stronger the launch or

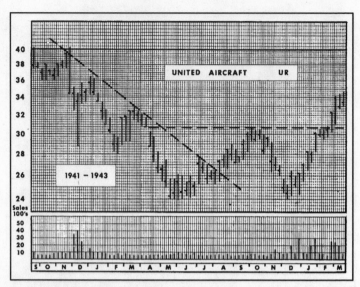

Figure 6.4   Double Bottom or "W" Pattern

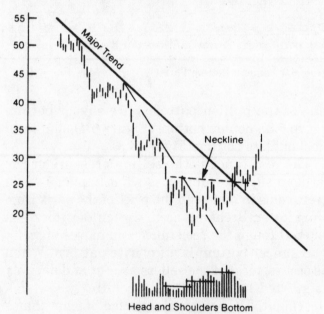

Figure 6.5   Head and Shoulders Bottom Pattern
(Courtesy of Alan Shaw)

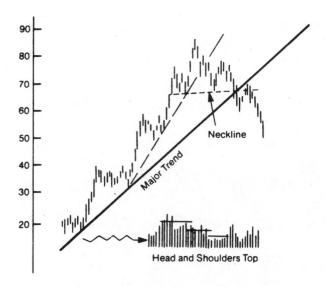

Figure 6.6 Head and Shoulders Top Pattern

breakout will be because the stock will have a firmer, stronger foundation or more support. This is true with any of the bullish patterns as shown in Figures 6.3 and 6.4 from *Technical Analysis of Stock Trends* by Robert D. Edwards and John Magee.

Figure 6.4 is called a double bottom. This is a "W" pattern. It has good support once it breaks through the top of the "W" or the resistance.

Figure 6.5, from Alan R. Shaw's *Technical Analysis*, is called a head and shoulders bottom and is also a strong pattern.

Bearish patterns exist and illustrate the picture of the supply and demand in negative markets as shown in 6.6, also from Shaw's *Technical Analysis*. A classic negative picture is a head and shoulders top (Figure 6.6). This looks exactly like a head with two shoulders. It shows massive overhead supply of stock that will come up for sale,

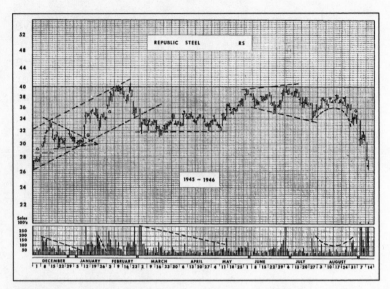

Figure 6.7 Double Top Pattern

since most market participants are trying to get their money back. This is the direct opposite of a head and shoulders bottom.

A double top (Figure 6.7) is our next chart (from *Technical Analysis of Stock Trends*). This is the opposite of a double bottom. This is an "M" pattern. When a stock drops below its neckline, it can take a long time to recover, and it generally drops lower before it recovers. This is a good reason to learn about charts and their patterns. They can keep you from losing a lot of money, as they will indicate when to get in and when to get out.

A rounded top (Figure 6.8, from *Technical Analysis of Stock Trends*) is another pattern that you will see. It is less common but is another sign of distribution, rather than accumulation, of stock.

There are many more patterns for both bearish and bullish markets, but the ones we have shown will give you a working knowledge of technical analysis and will enable you to carry on a knowledgeable conversation with your broker or other serious investors. If you are handling your account entirely on your own, further study is required. Whether you use a broker or not, you should subscribe to *Investor's Business Daily*. This paper is oriented toward technical analysis and contains a multitude of useful information. Another publication worthy of your subscription is *The Wall Street Journal*. It has long been a useful tool for investors and continues to be a good source of information.

Once you have a working knowledge of technical analysis and charts, there are three different

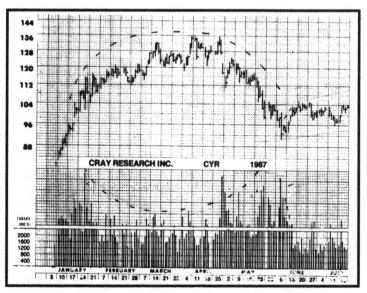

Figure 6.8 Rounded Top Pattern

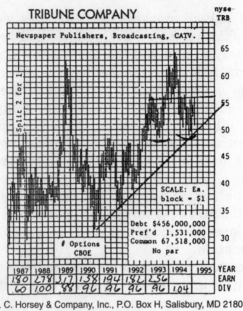

Source: M. C. Horsey & Company, Inc., P.O. Box H, Salisbury, MD 21801
(410) 742-3700.

Figure 6.9   Horsey Chart

perspectives that you should use to get a proper
view of supply and demand pictures. You should
look at long-term charts of ten years or longer. A
good one to consult is the Horsey Charts (Figure
6.9). You should also consider intermediate or
three-year charts. We suggest that you use the
Mansfield Charts (Figure 6.10) in this instance. In
fact, we suggest that you look at the Mansfield
Charts first for obviously strong technical patterns—for example, a saucer bottom. Finally, you
should consult short-term graphs such as the Daily
Graphs (Figure 6.11). These are one-year charts.
If you choose to work with a broker, ask him or her
to supply you with a copy of the Horsey, Mansfield,
and Daily Graphs on any stock that you are considering either buying or selling.

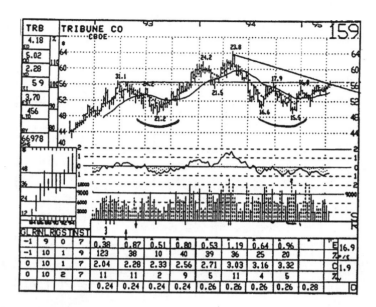

Figure 6.10

Not only can technical analysis indicate what stocks to buy and when, it can also show you when to sell and where to put your "stops." A stop loss can be entered at the time the stock is purchased. It is the point at which you want to sell a stock. You should purchase a stock as close as possible to the support. If you bought a stock at $20 per share and the support was also at $20, you may want to get out if it drops two points below the support or at $18 per share. If you entered a stop when you bought the stock, it will automatically be sold if it drops to $18 per share. (It is possible for the stock to close on one day at eighteen and one-half and reopen the next day at seventeen—in this case, your stock would be sold at the market value or seventeen.) If the $20 stock climbs to $26 per

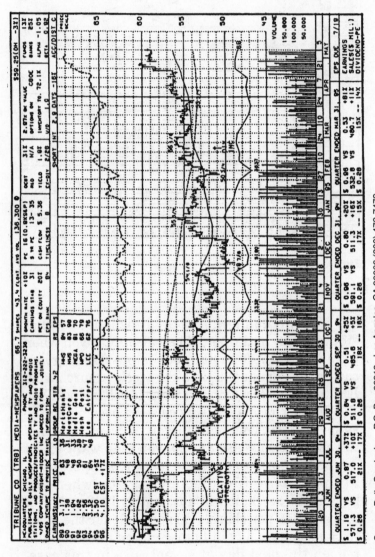

Source: Daily Graphs Inc., P.O. Box 66919, Los Angeles, CA 90066 (800) 472-7479.

Figure 6.11 Daily Graph

share, you probably would want to move the stop up so that you would not lose all of your profits if the stock turned down. If the resistance is at $25, you would move the stop to $23 per share. Stops, along with charts, help to remove the emotion from the decision of when to buy and when to sell. No system is perfect, but this is a discipline that works when you learn where to set your stops.

Again, to recap the discussion, use technical analysis to cut your losses short and to let your profits run. Stops remove the emotion. Investing is more factual than emotional. Technical patterns provide you with an opportunity to see firsthand what sophisticated investors are buying and selling. Smart money is always anticipating. Once the news is released, most of the money has been made.

Look for fundamental analysis only after the technicals point to a specific investment. The fundamentals will usually be improving at that time, and informed investors will be anticipating the fundamental improvement.

FUNDAMENTAL ANALYSIS

In order to properly analyze a company, you should also consider fundamental analysis. After the technicals point out a certain stock, check the fundamentals. To do this, you contemplate basic things. First, you should evaluate the industry. There are various sources that provide industry evaluations. *Value Line* is an independent publication that does a good job with evaluations. It is a good idea to ask your broker for evaluations from her or his research department as well. If they do not follow a specific stock, the broker should go outside the firm to find other research on the stock.

There are three sources of information that we consult when doing fundamental evaluations. First, look at a brokerage firm's research on the specific stock. Secondly, consult *Value Line*, which is particularly good at projecting the timeliness of a company and analyzing its safety. Both are broken down to a scale of one to five, with one being the highest and five the lowest. Look for a company with good future potential and an environment that allows high margins of profit or that lets a company raise prices based on its expenses. People in general are becoming "discount oriented." They are so used to going to discount food stores, discount furniture stores, or discount brokers that they are demanding value and services at reasonable prices. This is a long-term positive for the markets, both stocks and bonds. However, it will become increasingly important to be invested in companies with integrity and intelligent management. Profits should be a company's measurement of success, not its purpose. When you buy stocks, look for companies that are not susceptible to this pricing pressure, either because of lower costs or because they offer a unique service or product. You want to own a company that is making the highest percentage of profit possible.

Thirdly, examine the *Standard & Poor's Stock Reports*. It is also an excellent tool.

The earnings growth rate is also a factor to consider. A brokerage firm's research opinion will give average earnings estimates. Your broker has access to publications such as *Ibis* and *Zacks* that provide average estimates of earnings. Ask your broker for these. The actual earnings reported are not as important as the average expectation on Wall Street. You should buy when Wall Street's anticipations are low. Stan Weinstein often says, "It isn't the news, but how the market reacts to the news that's important." Watch how the stock reacts to earnings reports and other news events. If earnings are reported higher than the street's expectation, and your stock goes down, it might be advisable to review the fundamentals to determine if you want to sell and take your profits.

The price-to-earnings ratio (P/E ratio) is another element to examine. The price-to-earnings ratio should not exceed the company's growth rate. Do not place a lot of emphasis on this, other than just being aware of the two figures in order to compare them.

Warren Buffett, the king of fundamentalists, stresses the importance of return on equity (ROE) in a book written by Robert G. Hagstrom, Jr., *The Warren Buffett Way*. He considers this more important than the reported earnings per share. ROE is the actual percentage of return that management is making on the money it retains. Return on equity is the ratio of operating earnings to shareholders' equity. If the return on equity ratio is high, the next factor to consider is the amount of debt employed to achieve the return on equity. If the debt to capital figure is low and the return on equity is high, this adds strength to the fundamental position of the stock. You would also want to look at the amount of cash that the company generates. Find a company that has excess cash flow and low expenses and maintenance. For instance, a factory may have a huge cash flow but also has to maintain and replace or upgrade its equipment and pay its personnel. Compare that to a home shopping company that does not have to manufacture or maintain anything but also has a huge cash flow. The home shopping company would be the better company to purchase. Wall Street stresses earnings per share as opposed to return on equity. This will change in the future as people become more familiar with the ideas of sophisticated investors.

The management of a company is possibly the most important fundamental consideration for you. You can assume that a successful company has strong management, but for our purposes, it is best to assume nothing without thorough investigation. Look carefully at the management of a company. You want to see strength and a "hands-on" approach. Great companies have great managers. An example is the Walt Disney Company. Highly successful, strong management principles were established by Walt Disney and have been carried out and perfected by the current CEO, Michael Eisner.

Check the amount of money a company pays out in dividends. You want to see a steady increase in the dividend-paying history. Remember, though, growth stocks rarely pay high dividends.

Compare a company's current assets to its current liabilities. We prefer a two-to-one ratio or better. This information can be found in the *S&P Stock Guide* or in the *Standard & Poor's Stock*

Reports under the column Ratio. Your broker will have a copy. A company's current cash position is also relevant. This can also be found in the *S&P Stock Guide* and the *Standard & Poor's Stock Reports*.

We know there is a lot of information to master on stocks and selecting the best stocks. It has been said that we teach what we need to learn. Investing is an ongoing learning process for all. It is best to go over the information as many times as necessary until you feel comfortable with it. Perhaps you may want to select a couple of stocks, then follow them to see how you do. When you feel ready to enter the market, feel confident that you have learned your lessons well. Remember to follow your discipline of first checking the technicals, then the fundamentals. Define your risk, and if you make a mistake, know when to cut your losses. If you are correct, let your profits run. Be demanding and selective. It is better to own a few companies that meet your criteria than a large group of mediocre choices.

Now let's decide what percentage of your money should be invested in stocks (see Figure 6.12). We have used a positive environment for stocks as an example. Under those circumstances, we would recommend that the balance of your investment capital, with the exception of 5 percent, be invested in stocks. If we were in a negative environment, we would recommend reducing stock ownership and raising cash positions. You should evaluate your portfolio thoroughly. Other than a few possible core holdings, we would encourage you to have a substantial percentage of your stock

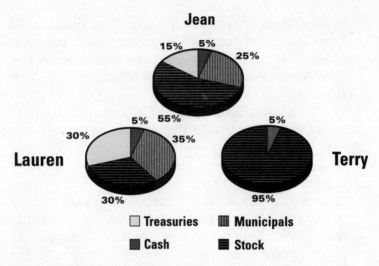

Figure 6.12   Positive Environment

allocations in cash or cash equivalents. At times, cash is the best asset class.

You have digested a vast amount of information. Like learning any art form or discipline, the basics or fundamentals can be a little tedious and redundant but actually participating can be exciting and invigorating. If necessary, ask for guidance as you begin your journey down Wall Street.

Let's recap what you have just learned.

SUMMARY

- The three things to consider before deciding to enter the stock market are interest rates (check the Monetary Pressure Index), market psychology (check the bullish and bearish consensus in *Investor's Business Daily*), and valuations (these can also be found in *Investor's Business Daily* on the same page as the bullish and bearish consensus).

- Review industry groups through technical analysis to determine areas of strength. Next, review technical patterns of individual stocks within the groups.

- Technical analysis is a chart of the supply and demand of a particular stock over a certain period of time. The patterns can be clearly bullish or bearish. The resistance is the selling pressure or the overhead supply. Support is what happens when buyers come in and keep a stock from falling lower. Breakout occurs when the stock has broken through the resistance and moves higher.

- Examples of technical bullish patterns are a saucer bottom, a double bottom, and a head and shoulders bottom .

- Examples of bearish patterns are a head and shoulders top, a double top, and a rounded top.

- Always look at three different time spans when using technical analysis—long-term or ten years or longer charts (Horsey Charts), intermediate or three-year charts (Mansfield Charts), and one-year charts (Daily Graphs).

- Technical analysis can help you determine where to put your stops when you purchase a stock.

- Look at the fundamental analysis only after the technicals point to a specific investment.

- With fundamental analysis you examine a company, hoping to find a high return on equity, a low percentage of debt, high net cash flows, high-quality management of the company, and a high ratio of current assets versus current liabilities.

- Look for companies that make a high margin of profit and can distinguish themselves from the competition.

That wraps up our discussion. By now the pieces should be falling into place. We sincerely hope that you master the information we are presenting to you, for we know the importance of your being informed, financially secure, and independent. It is exciting for us to know that you are getting closer and closer to your goal.

EVALUATING MONEY MANAGERS

"The whole investment management business together gives no value added. . . . That's the way it has to work."

— CHARLES T. MUNGER

Money managers are investment advisors with highly specialized styles and investment philosophies. They fashion their styles after a particular stock or bond class. Large-cap value managers or small-cap growth managers are two examples of management styles. A manager should have a clearly stated discipline to follow to achieve his client's desired results. Your broker should clearly understand your expectations so that he can pass the information along to the manager.

These accounts are not for everyone. Most money managers accept only accounts of $100,000 or more, although a few managers will accept accounts of $50,000. Also, many money managers work through brokerage firms, not directly with the individual. This will change someday, but now, the most effective way to choose a money manager is through a broker and a brokerage firm. A brokerage firm is able to screen money managers for you, so the current system is in your best interest, yet there is still room for improvement. If you want to select a money manager by yourself, there is an excellent publication available that conducts interviews with the top people in the field. It is entitled *Outstanding Investor Digest* and is based in New York City. We recommend this publication for anyone who is a serious student of the markets.

Most brokerage firms have analysts on staff who do nothing but familiarize themselves with money managers and evaluate their techniques. Money management is an area of rapid growth in the industry, and thus it will become more and more difficult to investigate each manager before one is selected.

Money managers are not financial planners. They do not set up budgets and savings plans or do retirement planning. They strictly invest your money.

Take responsibility for your own account. Too many people blindly pass that responsibility to others. If you have learned the criteria for selecting individual stocks and bonds, you are on your way to success in the markets. An uninformed broker may pass responsibility for your account to an inappropriate money manager or mutual fund. (A mutual fund is another form of money management that will be discussed in the next chapter.)

The money manager has never met you and does not have to answer to you directly. A frightening fact is that money managers get paid whether you make or lose money. This is a major flaw in the system.

Unless you have clearly defined investment objectives and the manager meets those standards, you will be better off in an S&P Index fund. An S&P Index fund is designed to represent the 500 stocks that make up the S&P 500. This index is composed of both growth and cyclical stocks and is less expensive than a money manager or a mutual fund since it is not actively managed.

Also unsettling is the fact that most money managers are not independent thinkers but rather part of the herd mentality, yet we give them our money anyway. It is a standing practice in the industry to first take a consensus of opinion from the money managers and then go the other direction. More often than not, at a critical turning point, the stock market and interest rates will have moved ahead of them. Some money managers do not have as strong a financial foundation as you will have after you have finished this book. Many are young, inexperienced people who have never lived through a prolonged downturn in the market. We give them our money to use to experiment. For them, it is like saying, "I want to learn to shave, and I'll learn on your legs." They are learning with your money and getting paid even when they lose money.

It is time for a shakeup in the industry. It needs a cleansing process. Individual investors must *demand* performance from their broker and manager. Informed clients will know enough to

question their broker or manager when in doubt.
What we are telling you is that ultimately
the responsibility falls on you, the investor. It is
your money.

Too many people on Wall Street are promot-
ing mediocrity. Just last week a principal of a
money management firm gave a presentation at
our brokerage office. He gave us a long speech on
"managing your clients' expectations." Clients who
had accounts with this firm last year averaged a
3 percent loss. He was telling us that the average
brokerage firm account was down 6 percent last
year, so the reality was that they were doing a
wonderful job. They were happy to lose 3 percent of
your money. Again, they were satisfied and brag-
ging about poor performance.

We contend that the reality is that every person who invests money expects to make money in
her account—not to lose less than some index.
Keep in mind that the more risk you are willing to
take in your account, the more likely the possibility that you will lose money. Risk and reward are
usually directly proportional.

There are some excellent managers available,
but the burden is on you to make sure you or your
broker select the right ones. Some people need to
invest with a money manager. People with a large
amount of money who are often unavailable when
decisions need to be made concerning their accounts do well with managers—if they are with the
right manager.

There are three areas of managed money that
have proffered better results than you can get with
your broker and at a lower cost. We will list these
and explain them in detail. First are fixed-income

taxable bond managers. Some of these managers are good if they are investing using the actively managed for total return method. Second are active asset allocators, some of whom add value and have produced good results. Their style is geared toward a more conservative client who wants to take less risk. They will make less in a bull market but also lose less in a down market. These managers will be explained in depth in the chapter on asset allocation. Third are a select few international managers, who serve a useful purpose as no one can know everything about every market. It is a form of specialization that can be valuable.

There are two types of money managers: fixed-income managers and equity or stock managers. Managers are either fixed-income managers, equity managers, or combinations of the two. *Fixed-income managers* deal in bond management. They charge lower fees than equity or stock managers, usually a percentage of the assets in your account. These usually start around $1\frac{1}{4}$ percent, but remember that these fees can be negotiated. As with bonds, there are two types of fixed-income management—taxable and nontaxable. Taxable managers invest in U.S. government and corporate securities. Tax-free managers invest in municipal bonds. You will recall from our discussion on bonds that municipal bonds are not as liquid as treasuries and corporates. The advice, based on personal experience, is to stay away from the tax-free managers.

Our second category of money managers is *equity or stock managers*. There are six different areas—value managers, growth managers, sector rotation managers, asset allocation managers, balanced managers, and international managers. Let's examine value managers first. **Value managers** invest in the stocks they consider to be undervalued. As you remember from our session on stocks, value stocks usually have a lower price-to-earnings ratio, are unloved and presently out of favor. Value managers attempt to buy low and sell higher. They invest in stocks, either large-cap, mid-cap, or small-cap. (See value investing in Step V if you need a review of this material.) Growth stocks can also be considered a value if they are out of favor, but generally this category is composed primarily of cyclical stocks.

Large-cap value managers look for stocks that offer a lower price-to-earnings ratio and usually pay higher dividends. A value manager tries to find stocks that are increasing their dividends, and he looks for improvements in earnings per share. These stocks have a lower five-year growth rate and are high-quality stocks. They also have a lower price-to-book value. Book value is computed by taking a company's assets, minus the liabilities, divided by the number of shares outstanding. Try to remember that book value is a relative term and should be scrutinized. A company's holdings can be misrepresented or misunderstood. For example, one company we looked at recently had real estate included as an asset on the books, but it was listed at today's perceived value instead of the price paid years earlier. Be cautious.

Small-cap cyclical stocks have characteristics similar to those of large-cap cyclicals, but the companies are smaller and more aggressive. They are more volatile than large-cap cyclicals, and with the higher risk comes higher returns. There are managers who specialize in this discipline. **Growth managers** purchase either large-cap growth stocks, mid-cap growth stocks, or small-cap growth stocks. To review, with large-cap growth stocks, usually the five-year earnings per share growth is high and steady, and likewise the return on equity should be high. They have either a low dividend or pay no dividend at all. Growth stocks generally exhibit a higher volatility than other types of stocks.

Small-cap growth managers are interchangeable with aggressive growth managers. They search for smaller companies than large-cap growth managers, which can be extremely volatile. These smaller companies experience the highest growth rate and have a high price-to-earnings ratio. They are usually smaller, non–S&P 500 companies. Small-cap growth stocks, according to the Ibbotson Chart, have the highest return. Refer to the Ibbotson Chart (Figure 5.1, page 59).

Although small-cap growth stocks are perceived to have the highest return, look at Figure 7.1. It shows the actual return from December 1975 through March 1995. On average, the smaller cap stocks did not fare as well as other investments. This is a case of discrepancy between fact and perception and also risk and reward. High-quality mature companies can provide excellent returns with less risk. The *Value Line Index* was used because the *Russell 2000 Index* has not been in existence for the entire time period examined. The *Value Line Index* is a broader index and contains many small-cap companies.

Nineteen-Year Return from December 1975 to March 1995

7.23%	9.40%	11.90%	13.88%	7.70%	15.08%
Treasury Bill	Intermediate Treasuries	Combination of Intermediate Treasuries and Large-Cap Stocks	Large-Cap Stocks S&P 500	Small-Cap Stocks Value Line Index	International

Figure 7.1   Nineteen-Year Return Chart

Keep in mind that these returns are computed before taxes and inflation have been considered. (Refer to Figure 7.2.) Treasury bills actually provide a negative return when these are subtracted.

Sector rotation managers are our third group. They do less stock picking and are more concerned with being in the right industry at the right time. They will move from industry to indus-

TREASURY BILLS "RETURN FREE" INVESTING?

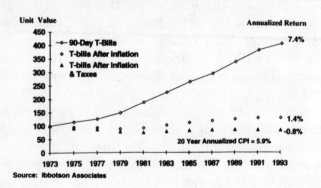

Source: Ibbotson Associates

Figure 7.2

try according to their outlook on the economy. We are not recommending this type of management for any of you. The danger is that they may be in the wrong place at the wrong time. When they are right, they can be highly effective. Again, you must take the responsibility for knowing what is going on in your own account. If you learn all of the material that we have given you, you will know enough to protect yourself in most situations.

Asset allocation managers are next. We will have an entire chapter on asset allocation, but let's just hit the high points here. Asset allocation managers make bold portfolio movements. They could be 100 percent in stocks or 100 percent in cash if they feel the market is vulnerable. They base decisions first on the economic outlook, then on stock selections. Asset allocators usually use technical analysis more than fundamental analysis. They tend to stay very liquid, so they invest in large, capitalized companies for ease in market entrance and exit. They are considered to be far more conservative investors, because they will attempt to go to cash in a down market so you will not lose your money; however, in an up market they will make less. This management style is an excellent choice for a person who wants growth but is risk averse. There is a risk with this type of management that the manager will miss a major move in the overall market, either up or down.

Balanced managers manage stocks and bonds in the same portfolio. This too is a conservative approach, because the income earned from bonds will cushion the investor in a market downturn. If you are concerned about preserving principal and need growth, this is another appropriate form of management. Again, be very selective. It is less expensive to hire a separate bond manager and an equity manager. Separate managers have more expertise in their respective fields, although the two areas must be coordinated. A balanced manager who effects the proper allocation between bonds and stocks can be of significant value. These accounts need to be actively managed.

Lastly we should look at *international managers*. They invest primarily in American Depository Receipts (ADRs) of foreign corporations. They can be either value or growth style managers. International managers can reduce risk over the long term through diversification when combined with a U.S. equity manager. Historically, these managers provide the highest returns, but they are also perceived to have the highest risk. Most people do not think they know as much about the international markets, and they are constantly being affected by currency fluctuations. International managers can handle either of two types of portfolios: global portfolios and strictly international investments. Global portfolios consist of U.S. equities and offshore investments. In some markets this is the best method; however, when the U.S. market is weak, it may pay to be more heavily invested in international holdings.

There are advantages to using a money manager. These people are highly specialized in a particular style of stock or bond investing, and they are very focused in that area. With a managed money account, the client owns individual stocks and bonds, not shares in a pooled account. Since the investor owns individual shares, she is not subject to forced redemptions like mutual funds.

Mutual fund managers are often forced to buy and sell at the wrong time. In a bad market, people will want to get out of a mutual fund, so the mutual fund manager is forced to liquidate shares to pay them. This forces the mutual fund manager to sell at what may be the bottom of the market. When the market is up and people are buying more shares of mutual funds, the manager is forced to buy shares near the top of the market. With a money manager, you have an individual account, and you can ultimately make your own decisions about when to open or liquidate this account. There is no penalty for closing out a managed money account.

Fees are prorated. There are two kinds of fees. The most common is a wrap fee. This is a fee that includes management fees and commissions. It is paid quarterly regardless of the number of trades, and it usually starts at 3 percent of the assets in your account, but it also can be negotiated. In the future, fees should drop as competition increases and informed investors demand higher returns. In addition to the management fees, execution charges are also charged on every transaction. In a poorly managed account, these can amount to several percent. Be aware of these because the wrong manager can cost you money. The other kind of fee is a separate management fee plus commission. These are less common.

You should make decisions on managers according to your goals and risk tolerance. Your broker should point you in the right direction and to the appropriate type of manager for your needs, since styles of management often fall in and out of favor for long periods of time. You should not select a particular manager based on high returns, because each manager will excel in a market that is favorable to his or her individual style. Extremely high performance is usually indicative of high risk. Again, consider your goals and tolerance for risk before finalizing this decision. It is a good idea to look back over a manager's past performance. See how he or she has performed in down markets. If you can live with the results in bad markets, then you will most likely be able to stay with the program long enough to make money.

You may be wondering why you would need a money manager. Your broker may always have taken care of you, and you may trust her or him completely. Your broker may care about what happens to you and your family. A money manager would not even know you. Why would a money manager care if you lost money? He or she would be making a fee anyway.

However, there are times when hiring a money manager would be a prudent decision. Do you feel capable of making your own decision on an individual stock? Before you started learning about investing, you conceivably could not have made a sound decision on a stock or bond selection. However, now, not only can you evaluate a stock but you would most likely welcome the opportunity. You are learning a lot and are probably anxious to put your new knowledge to work. Before you start investing, there are a few more points to consider.

There are other instances when a manager would be beneficial for you. If you wanted to diversify your holdings, you might want to invest some money with an international manager. Or if you are not comfortable remaining fully invested in the market at all times, a good asset allocation manager would move you from stocks to bonds to cash as he or she saw fit. If you had a core group of stocks that you had bought over the years that you intended to hold for a long time, we would not recommend that you use a money manager. Just remember that there can be long periods of time when financial markets perform poorly.

In Lauren's case, we might recommend that she invest a small percentage of her money with a taxable fixed-income (bond) manager who manages for total return. These managers actively manage their accounts and trade often. It would be cost prohibitive to pay individual commissions on all of these trades. They are constantly monitoring the bond market—a broker could not devote the same amount of time to this one market.

Let's take a look at money managers for Terry. We would not think that an individually managed account is for her. The $100,000 minimum account would either exclude her or limit her diversification too much. She would be better off to invest in mutual funds. We will discuss these in depth in the next chapter.

Jean wanted to learn about investments so she could handle her family's investments herself. She now feels capable of making individual stock or bond decisions, as long as she can still discuss her decisions with a knowledgeable broker. She has the knowledge; now the confidence will come with experience and success.

If we were handling Jean's account, we would suggest that she invest approximately 20 percent of her stock allocation with an international manager. This will allow her more diversification. We would also suggest that the 15 percent of her money that is allocated for U.S. treasuries be invested with a taxable fixed-income manager for the same reasons that we cited for Lauren. Since she does not need income and is investing that portion of her bond money for total return, meaning that she is reinvesting her income received on the bonds plus any appreciation in order to achieve a conservative growth of capital, a manager can best facilitate this.

Let's summarize.

SUMMARY

- Money managers are investment advisors with highly specialized styles and investment philosophies.
- There are two categories of money managers—fixed-income or bond managers and equity or stock managers.
- Fixed income managers handle bonds. There are two types: taxable and nontaxable. Some taxable managers add value to your account, but we do not recommend tax-free managers.
- There are six types of equity managers: value managers, growth managers, sector rotation managers, asset allocation managers, balanced managers, and international managers.
- When using a money manager, a client owns individual stocks and bonds, not shares in a pooled account.

- Fees are prorated, and the wrap fee is the most commonly used.
- There is no penalty for closing out an account.
- Accounts must be $100,000 or more. A client should work with her broker to select a manager according to her own goals and risk tolerance.
- Your broker should advise you on the right type of manager, because styles of management often fall in and out of favor—just remember, the final decision is up to you.

If you are comfortable with the information on money managers, we will move on to explain mutual funds.

SELECTING
MUTUAL FUNDS

*"Knowledge paves the road to riches—
when you know which road to take."*
—NAPOLEON HILL

Mutual funds can be a confusing topic. When starting to gather and organize the material on mutual funds, we called the Securities and Exchange Commission to get their information on the topic. When the information arrived, we were even more discomfited. Mutual funds have grown so fast over the last few years that the SEC is concerned and soliciting input from investors to clarify certain areas. There are now more mutual funds than there are stocks on the New York Stock Exchange. Included in the Security and Exchange Commission's information packet was a questionnaire asking for investor suggestions on how to improve the descriptions of risk in mutual funds.

The risk versus reward of investing in a mutual fund is explained in a written prospectus furnished by the mutual fund itself. It also contains information about the fund's costs, risks, past performance, and investment goals and is helpful in selecting the appropriate mutual fund. Make sure these goals match your own before purchasing the mutual fund.

There is a problem with this method of informing the investor. You must request a copy of the prospectus prior to purchasing shares in the mutual fund, and then the burden is on you to read the information. Investors rarely read prospectuses, because they are long and difficult to understand. In order to help you clarify your goals and the amount of risk you can comfortably withstand, we have devised a checklist to consider before buying a mutual fund. The SEC has asked investors if they would like prospectuses to contain a summary of risk. This is an excellent idea, but to date it is unavailable. Let's look at the questions.

1. What percentage of your total liquid assets is going into this fund? The larger the percentage you invest, the less risk you would want to take. The older you are, the less risk you would want to accept because it would be more difficult for you to replace these assets. Give this careful thought.

2. How long are you going to hold this mutual fund? A complete market cycle is three years. If you do not plan to hold your investment for at least three years, you should

not be in a mutual fund. Your investment time frame should fall into one of three classifications: three to five years, five to ten years, or ten years or longer.

3. Do you have a particular goal for these funds, such as funding college educations, retirement, a new home, building wealth, or some other goal?

4. Do you need income from this money? If so, do you need tax-free income, taxable income, or total return (a combination of price appreciation and income, usually to be reinvested)?

5. What volatility are you willing to accept over your chosen time horizon? Volatility is the fluctuation in the market, either up or down. This can affect you if you have to sell sooner than your anticipated time horizon. Before you buy any investment, you should know how much you are willing to lose if you have to sell early. Decide what percentage of your money you are comfortable risking. (Pick a figure: Is it 0 percent, 5 percent, 15 percent, 20 percent? Now convert that percentage into a dollar figure so you are entirely aware of the amount.)

6. Look at the cost structure (this can include sales loads and management fees) based on the time period that you plan to hold the fund. This will help you decide whether to buy A, B, C, or no-load shares. For example, if your time horizon is ten years or longer, you would save money if you purchased A shares. These will be explained shortly.

The following checklist should help you to evaluate the amount of risk you are willing to take. We have put together a Risk Line Chart showing the amount of risk involved in various investments. Find yourself on the chart based on the *percentage of money* (see the Percentage of Risk table, Figure 8.1, below) that you can tolerate losing. No one ever wants to lose money, but you have to understand that it can happen. If you do not want any risk, you should invest in a money market deposit account, certificates of deposit, or treasury bills. Just remember that there is also the risk of being too conservative and not meeting your retirement needs or other goals. Now, in order to be realistic about what kind of a return you can expect, look at the chart, entitled Nineteen-Year Return (on page 104). If you look at treasury bills on the chart you will see that historically they offer a 7.23 percent annual return before taxes and inflation. Keep in mind that these figures will vary from year to year. We are talking about averages. Once you have found your category on the Percentage of Risk table, move on to the Risk Line Chart (Figure 8.2).

Next, based on your risk category—either low, medium, or high—find your appropriate invest-

---

Percentage of Risk

0 to 10%	Low risk
11 to 15%	Medium risk
16% and up	High risk

Figure 8.1

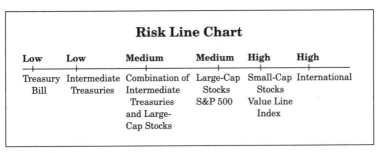

Figure 8.2

ment choices and their average return, using the Nineteen-Year Return chart on page 104.

Now that you have some idea as to the amount of risk you can tolerate and an average of the amount of return that corresponds to the level of risk, let's go on to our explanation of mutual funds. Mutual funds are investments that pool your money with the money of other investors. There are advantages to pooling assets. It allows you to participate in the greater buying power of the fund, and you have to invest only small increments of money. It is more cost effective to buy larger quantities of stocks and bonds. Mutual funds allow you to diversify. If you cannot buy ten stocks in your individual portfolio, you may be better off in a mutual fund. They also provide professional management. This can be an advantage if you choose the proper fund manager.

Two basic kinds of mutual funds exist: open-end mutual funds and closed-end mutual funds. Open-end funds are the most common type. They issue shares on a continuing basis. The number of shares increases as money comes into the fund. The number of shares decreases as shares are redeemed. The Net Asset Value (NAV) per share is the value of one share in a fund. A fund's NAV will fluctuate daily.

There are four major types of mutual funds: *money markets, bond funds, balanced funds, and stock funds*. **Money markets** are low-risk, highly liquid investments. You can usually draw checks against these funds. For every dollar invested, you get one dollar in return plus the interest earned on the pool of short-term income securities in the fund. Money market accounts can be taxable or tax free depending on where the money is invested. Taxable funds are invested in short-term U.S. government securities (treasury bills, for example) or corporate short-term debt (commercial paper, for example).

Tax-free money markets are limited to short-term municipal debt. You can buy money market funds for states with unusually high taxes such as New York or California. Your interest would be tax-free in those states or municipalities where you reside. Compare the after-tax yield of tax-free funds with taxable funds to determine the best place to put your money. (See Step IV, page 50.)

Bond funds are our next type of mutual fund. One can choose different length maturities for the bonds in which bond fund managers invest. A short-term investment would be from one to five years. Intermediate-term would range from five to ten years. Long-term investments can extend thirty years or more. Do not get confused here. There is no actual maturity date for shares of the fund—just the bonds held in the fund. The investor has a choice of whether to reinvest the income earned or to receive a monthly check.

High yield is another name for junk bond funds. We want to touch on these just so you will understand what they are, but we are not advocating that you purchase these for your account. These are low-grade corporate bonds. Remember, if the yield sounds too good to be true, it probably is. There are two types of bond funds, *taxable and tax free*. Taxable funds can be invested in U.S. government securities, corporate securities, or a combination of the two. It is important for you to know why you are placing your money in a fund in order to pick the appropriate one for your needs. For example, do you need monthly income, or do you need to save money on your taxes? You cannot always choose a fund based on the material that looks obvious. We recall a situation that occurred at a major brokerage firm. The firm established a mutual fund and called it a retirement fund. Initially, this fund was used primarily for IRAs and retirement accounts. However, upon closer evaluation, it was clear to see that it was composed of growth stocks and was a very aggressive fund. It has been a successful investment for numerous clients inside and outside of their retirement accounts, and it has performed beautifully, but a client seeking a conservative retirement fund should never have bought it. The name was misleading. A few years later they changed the name.

With today's multitude of mutual funds, it is necessary to become more and more inquisitive before investing your money. The bottom line here is to do your homework: know why you are purchasing and what the fund is buying. It is always a good idea to ask your broker to pull the top ten holdings of any mutual fund that he or she is proposing. You want to also make sure that you do not have a lot of overlap of stocks in the various funds that you own. The point is to own quality companies that you like and to have proper diversification. You should choose mutual funds with the same selectivity and high standards you use in picking stocks.

You may come across some nebulous terms when you start your investing. Just be sure that you ask questions so you understand what terms such as *good growth, strong growth, low risk, blue chip, high income,* and *capital appreciation* mean. These terms can mean different things to different people.

Another important fact to be aware of is that you can shorten or extend bond maturities within the same family of funds without being charged a fee. If your broker calls you to tell you that interest rates are going to go down and you would do well to extend maturities from short term to intermediate term, know that there need not be a fee involved in this transaction. You may be able to achieve the desired results by merely extending maturities within the same family of funds. Then you can avoid paying an additional fee. Be aware that the switch may generate capital gains or losses. You should always examine switching within the same family of funds prior to selling one fund and purchasing another.

Tax-free funds are our second category of bond funds. They are invested in municipal bonds. There are times when you would want to purchase this type of bond fund.

A situation that you might want to keep in

mind is that if several new mutual fund offerings of the same type are brought to market at about the same time, it may be a sign of a "market top" in that segment of the marketplace. A "market top" is the saturation point where supply is greater than demand. The investment community is predictable. It will inevitably rush to create products to meet the public's demand—especially in "hot" investment sectors of the market. Remember, as demand increases, supply also increases, and eventually prices will go down. Think independently and do not get caught up in the current of public opinion, because the majority is usually wrong.

Another type of mutual fund is called a **balanced fund**. The manager of this fund invests in both stocks and bonds. This type of fund is considered to be more conservative, since the investor will continue to earn interest on the bond portion of the fund even if the stock market goes down.

The final category of mutual funds is **stock funds**. Managers of stock funds have a specific style of investing or a discipline that they use. You should focus on your goals and use the proper mix of stock funds. Management styles fall in and out of favor, and favorable performance can depend on being in the right place at the right time. There are six primary types of stock funds and managers: *growth, value, index, sector, global,* and *international.*

Since you now understand growth stocks, understanding growth funds will be simple. **Growth funds** may also be called appreciation funds. These terms are not interchangeable, because appreciation funds may also contain cyclical stocks. Aggressive growth funds are very volatile. They are composed of small-cap growth stocks. As you remember from our section on growth stocks, they are stocks with a steadily growing earning stream—regardless of the economic environment. Growth stocks have a high price-to-earnings ratio, and they work well in a buy and hold philosophy. Investors in small-cap growth stock funds must either have long time horizons or perfect timing. The conventional wisdom on Wall Street is that small-cap growth stocks outperform all other areas. According to the Value Line Index, looking back to December 1975, this has not been the case. Smaller cap stocks averaged a 7.7 percent return. A no-risk treasury bill investment, over the same time period, averaged a 7.23 percent return. Again, learn to challenge the conventional wisdom.

Mid-cap growth funds are composed of stocks of medium-sized companies. There is less risk with mid-cap stocks but also the possibility of less return.

Finally, there are large-cap growth funds. These funds are composed of stocks of large, mature, well-known companies. These stocks have moderate risk, and growth is steady in all economic environments. They rarely pay a high dividend but rather reinvest the profits or earnings of the company back into the company. These are often referred to as blue chip stocks. Remember that although the growth is steady, the market may not value growth at this particular time, and excellent growth stocks will be sluggish and underperform.

Value funds are our second type of stock funds. Value funds invest in value stocks. Again, "value" is a nebulous term. Look further to be aware of what you are buying in a value fund. Remember that with value investing, you are investing in companies that are perceived to be unloved or out of favor. Generally there are more cyclical stocks in this category, but there can also be out of favor growth stocks. The concept of value investing is based on the premise of buying low so that you can sell high. These stocks can be either small-cap, mid-cap, or large-cap value stocks. They have a low price-to-earnings ratio and usually pay a high dividend. They are often perceived to be less volatile than growth stock funds.

Index funds are the third type of stock fund. They purchase shares of stock in companies listed in a specific index such as the S&P 500. The fund's performance should mirror the index's performance. Management fees for index funds should be lower than those for other stock funds. This is a good place for most investors who cannot afford to buy a diversified portfolio or do not have the necessary expertise to make the selections.

Sector funds are the fourth type of stock fund. Managers of these funds invest in a specific industry. They are advocates of the market timing philosophy, meaning that they try to time the cycles of the economy so that they can be in the right industry at the right time. This is very difficult to do effectively and is not for everyone. However, it can be very rewarding if it is done correctly. A sector fund manager could alternate holdings between precious metal funds composed of gold and silver shares and a natural resources fund that may hold stocks in oil, gold, silver, or forest products. Other industries in which they may invest are airlines, technology, health care, and housing. Our advice to you would be to stay away from this type of fund. There are other places to invest your money that are more secure.

Global funds are our fifth type of mutual stock fund. They allow you diversification in markets other than just the U.S. market. Global fund managers invest in U.S. stocks and also non-U.S. stocks. These managers can invest using either growth or value styles.

Our sixth, and last, type of mutual stock are **international funds**. Managers of these funds invest only in non-U.S. stocks. There is a place for this type of fund in nearly every person's portfolio. If the United States is experiencing a bad market, you might do well in an international market.

Closed-end funds are not encountered as often as open-end funds. In the case of closed-end funds, shares are issued just one time and are then traded on a major exchange like the New York Stock Exchange just like an individual stock. Country funds, such as the Japan Equity Fund, sometimes work this way.

Again, you should purchase funds to achieve a specific goal. In order to realistically evaluate a fund, you must examine its costs. Costs consist of sales loads and management fees and can be used in various combinations. All funds have management fees, but not all funds charge loads.

- Front-end loads are A shares. With this type of sales load you pay the costs up front. You should stay in this type of fund for six years or longer. For example, you might buy A shares to fund a child's college education.

- Back-end loads are called B shares. When using this structure, you pay a deferred load when you sell the fund. It is a declining back-end load, which means that the longer you hold the fund, the less of a sales load you will have to pay. Twelve B-1 fees are charged annually on back-end load funds.

  Make sure you know how much you are paying with these types of fees, because they can be expensive. These fees are most often used to pay commissions to brokers and other salespeople. They are usually between one-quarter of 1 percent and 1 percent annually. All mutual funds have ongoing expenses, and these are charged to the client in the form of an annual management fee. The management fee is a percentage of the assets in the account.

- C shares have no front-end load but do have a higher management fee. If you plan to hold the fund for five years or more, a front-end load may be better. These are sometimes called level-load funds. You pay a percentage of the assets annually plus management fees.

- No-loads do not charge sales loads. There is no assistance from a professional in this type of fund—you are on your own and have to make your own decisions. Examine the management fees carefully, because if there is no sales load, they have to pay for the marketing expenses somehow.

- Brokers should clearly explain the type of fees and loads that you are paying. They should give you the net cost so that you know where you stand. The SEC cautions investors: "Beware of a salesperson who tells you, 'This is just like a no-load fund.' Even if there is a front-end load, check the fee table in the prospectus to see what other loads or fees you may have to pay. Check the fee table to see if any part of a fund's fees or expenses has been *waived*. If so, the fees and expenses may increase suddenly when the waiver ends (the part of the prospectus after the fee table will tell you by how much)."

• Most funds allow you to exchange your shares for shares of another fund managed by the same family of funds. The first part of the fee table will tell you if there is any *exchange fee*.

We would be remiss if we did not hammer home the following very important point. We briefly mentioned fund switching, but this is an exceedingly significant concept. There is usually little or no fee if you switch from one fund to another, as long as you stay within the same family of funds. Before selling and buying a new fund for a different purpose, you should always look for alternatives in your present family of funds.

Churning of mutual funds in order to generate commissions is an infrequent event that does exist in spite of industry efforts to stop it. The sad fact about this is that the victims are usually trusting people who can least afford it. Anyone who has been in the business for any period of time has most likely run across one of the unethical brokers who does this. They often target an uninformed woman. The brokerage firm becomes aware of these parasites because they generate large amounts of commission on moderate amounts of assets. What some do is prey on retired, trusting, elderly women on fixed incomes and charge them unnecessary fees and commissions. The management will eventually drive the unscrupulous brokers out, but the frightening fact is that often these brokers are still working in the system. Often before the brokerage firm has enough ammunition to terminate these brokers, they will move to another brokerage firm and continue their abhorrent behavior. The brokerage firms are afraid of lawsuits and find it difficult to terminate these employees. Also, clients are reluctant to come forward and air their problems.

Please do not think that brokers are evil people who are out to get you. This is not the case. The overwhelming majority of brokers are good, caring, and competent professionals. It is always better to know the dangers of a worse case scenario—then you will be cautious.

If you happen to encounter a problem or have a question about a mutual fund, contact an SEC consumer specialist. To find the branch office nearest you, contact:

U.S. Securities and Exchange
Commission Headquarters

> Office of Consumer Affairs
> 450 Fifth Street NW
> Washington, DC 20549
> (202) 942-7040

Caution should be used against investing with a rearview mirror. This means you should not select a mutual fund because it did well last quarter. Do not select a fund based solely on past performance or pick last quarter's "hot" fund. Instead, check the fund's *total return*. The SEC informs us that you will find it in the *Financial Highlights*, near the front of the prospectus. They also suggest looking at variations in total return over a ten-year period. One good year followed by several mediocre years does not make something a good investment. The SEC recommends, "Looking at year-to-year changes in total return is a good way to see how stable the fund's returns have been."

We want to emphasize the point that the SEC stresses in their pamphlet *Invest Wisely*. Banks now sell mutual funds. Do not think that just because you are buying the mutual fund from a bank that the fund is FDIC insured. This insurance is only for deposits. Likewise, a money market fund is a type of mutual fund, and even though it is sold by a bank, it is not guaranteed. Do not confuse this with a money market deposit account. This is a bank deposit and is guaranteed. A money market deposit comes with a *Truth in Savings* form. A money market fund comes with a prospectus.

The future of mutual funds is going to be an interesting subject to follow. We believe there will be some changes in this industry. Mutual funds are going to have to be more tightly regulated. This area of investments has grown excessively large in a relatively short period of time. The SEC is examining the risk of mutual funds. The funds need to provide a clear projection of risk to the investor. As it stands now, there is a vast amount of information that is rapidly available to the investor through the use of computers and printed material, but it needs to be organized in an easy to use format.

Considering all of the information on fees and brokers' commissions, it is interesting to note the results of a study conducted by DALBAR Financial Services, Inc., entitled *1993 Quantitative Analysis of Investor Behavior.* When considering the actual rate of return for the period from January 1984 to September 1993, investors who purchased funds from brokers, or sales force purchases, outperformed the direct market funds, or no-load fund purchases. (See Figure 8.3.)

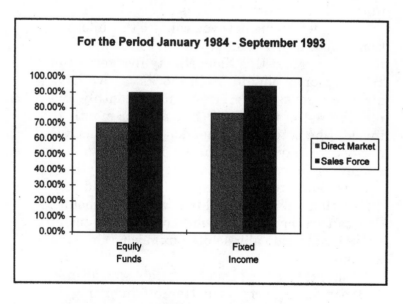

Figure 8.3   *Investor Performance Cumulative Real Investor Return*

The study found that sales force–advised investors outperformed direct market investors by over 20 percent in equity and 14 percent in fixed-income funds. The difference in results is directly attributable to longer retention periods and reduced reaction to changes in market conditions. The brokers tended to hold the funds for longer periods of time. The brokers' buy and hold philosophy outperformed the average individual investor's attempts to trade mutual funds by more than three to one after ten years. Individual investors have increased assets in direct market or no-load funds where they perform the worst, and assets have declined in areas where direct market or no-load investors perform best. An investor should weigh all of the facts before investing in a no-load fund to determine if it really is a bargain.

Let's determine how you can use this information in your own accounts. We will consider Terry's investments first this time. Ninety-five percent of Terry's money should be in stocks, as we have already discussed. Terry gets paid monthly and has figured out that she has $200 a month to invest. She is to be commended because she has decided to pay herself first—or put aside the money for investing and saving before anything else is paid. She has carefully budgeted and knows that she can afford to invest this amount. (You can arrange to have your monthly investment amount automatically debited from your checking account.)

Since this is not enough to establish a diversified portfolio, Terry is better off investing in mutual funds. She needs to "dollar cost average." This means that she needs to invest the same dollar amount in mutual funds every month, regardless of what is happening in the market. We would recommend that she put $150 per month in an S&P 500 Index fund. This is a fund consisting of large-cap stocks, both growth and cyclicals, that are S&P 500 companies. The other $50 a month should go to an international mutual fund. Terry is young, and she can handle the risk. The historic returns over the last nineteen years have proven these two investments to be superior to all other options.

Jean had a total of $500,000. We have decided that one-half of her money should be invested in stocks. Jean should buy large-cap stocks, S&P 500 companies, either in individual stocks or as part of a mutual fund. If she has the time to spend and the desire to invest individually, she would enjoy selecting her own stocks. Jean should put 15 percent of her stock money, or $37,500, in an international mutual fund.

Lauren is in the enviable position of having a total of $2 million to invest. Of that money, we have allocated $600,000 for her stock portfolio. Out of her stock allocation, she invests 10 percent, or $60,000, in an international mutual fund.

Let's summarize.

SUMMARY

- Mutual funds are investments that pool your money with that of other investors.
- Consider this six-point checklist before buying a mutual fund:

1. What percentage of your total assets are going into the fund?
2. How long are you going to hold the fund?
3. Do you have a particular goal for these funds?
4. Do you need income from this money?
5. What volatility are you willing to accept over your chosen time horizon?
6. Examine the cost structure based on the time period that you plan to hold the funds.

- Open end mutual funds are the most common. The number of shares is directly proportional to the amount of money going into or out of the fund.
- There are four types of open-end mutual funds: *money market funds*, *bond funds*, *balanced funds*, and *stock funds*.
- Funds invested in bonds can be either taxable or tax free. Know why you are purchasing the fund and what you hope to accomplish.
- There are six types of stock funds depending on the type of stocks that are held within a fund: *growth funds*, *value funds*, *index funds*, *sector funds*, *global funds*, and *international funds*.
- Closed-end funds are not common. They issue shares one time and then trade on a major stock exchange, just like an individual stock.

- Examine risk versus reward before buying any mutual fund.

- Know the fees and sales loads you are going to pay before you purchase any fund. These will affect your return.

- Remember that it is often possible to switch a fund within the same family of funds without paying additional fees or commissions.

- Do not select a mutual fund because it had one good year. Look long-term and compare the returns. Do your homework.

We have a very interesting topic, asset allocation, to look forward to in the next chapter. Now that you know what types of investments are available, you need to examine when and how much to invest in each.

DETERMINING YOUR ASSET ALLOCATION

"Never follow the crowd."
—*BERNARD BARUCH*

Asset allocation is the single most important decision that you make regarding your investments. Ninety-one and one-half percent of portfolio performance comes from asset allocation. Asset allocation is the distribution of your money among the asset classes in order to achieve your desired investment results.

This information will be simplified as much as possible so that you have an uncomplicated, workable discipline to follow when trying to determine what to do and when to do it. The first thing to remember is that there are three asset classes: stocks, bonds, and cash or cash equivalents. Stocks are the most volatile asset class, bonds have a moderate risk factor, and cash or cash equivalents would be considered to have little or no risk. Every investment that we are discussing is going to involve one of these three asset classes or combinations of the three.

Let's assume that you have never invested before and you have to allocate your money between the three asset classes. Before you can decide how to allocate your money, you must first have an opinion about the present monetary environment. Do we have a positive or negative environment? Remember when we mentioned the Monetary Pressure Index? Now is the time to apply it to asset allocation. If you are controlling your own asset allocation, study and monitor the index regularly. When the Monetary Pressure Index makes a move or turns in the opposite direction, you will likewise want to make adjustments in your holdings.

Trends tend to last for quite some time, with positive markets usually lasting longer than negative ones. We recommend that you make a habit of checking the index, or its equivalent, so that you do not miss the trend change. If your broker is with one of the other major brokerage firms, urge him to monitor the monetary environment and his firm's recommended asset allocation for you. All major brokerage firms make asset allocation recommendations. Please keep in mind that the following recommendations as to asset allocation are our personal opinions—not those of any specific brokerage firm.

Now that you know the present market environment, the next thing to consider is your individual risk tolerance. We discussed this in our chapter on mutual funds. Remember when we asked you to consider the percentage of money that you were willing to lose? Then we told you to convert it to a dollar figure so that you knew exactly the amount that you were talking about. There are various things to consider when arriving at a figure. You should take your age into consideration. As you get older, you should take less risk. You should also consider things such as your earning power. If you lose your money, do you have the ability to replace it? After you have established your figure and percentage, look on the Percentage of Risk table (on page 116) to determine what investments fit your profile.

Now that you have determined whether you should be in low-, medium-, or high-risk investments, look at the Risk Line Chart (on page 117) to determine what investments should be in your portfolio.

There is one other important consideration. What are your investment goals? Do you need income from your investments to support yourself? Are you saving and investing for a specific purpose like retirement or to pay for your children's college educations? Some people invest for a specific purchase like a new home or a special vacation. Whatever your goals happen to be, they are important in determining your investment strategy. For instance, if you are investing Christmas bonus money or savings for a trip to Europe in July, you probably would not enter the stock market.

Now that you have established the monetary environment, your personal risk tolerance, and your investment goals, you need to be aware that different strategies work better in different markets. If we have a positive environment, stocks and bonds should both do well. As the environment changes from negative to positive, the bonds will move up first, and the stocks usually follow. At this point, bonds might be a better relative value to stocks. If so, you need to weight your portfolio toward bonds. If our monetary index turns down, we would advise that you raise cash. Some people do not consider cash to be an asset class; however, in a negative market, it is the best asset class to have.

We want to personalize this for you. We have given you a breakdown of the disbursement of investments in a positive market for each of the composite women (Figure 9.1). It is in chart form so that it is easy to understand. Look at how allocations would need to change if the Monetary Pressure Index indicated that we were in a negative market (Figure 9.2).

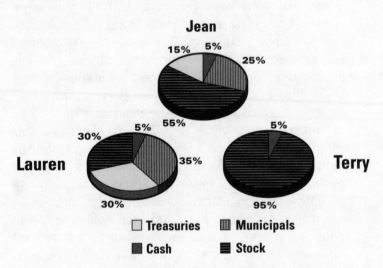

Figure 9.1   Asset Allocation in a Positive Monetary Environment

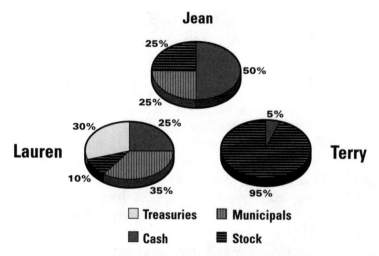

Figure 9.2   Asset Allocation in a Negative Environment

It is interesting to look at how asset allocation changes based on the monetary environment. Look at Lauren's investments first. Lauren has assets totaling $2 million. Remember that Lauren has to live on the income of her investments, so it is important that she maintain her principal and income. In a negative environment, Lauren would keep the disbursement the same in treasuries and municipal debt—maintaining 30 percent, or $600,000, in treasuries and 35 percent, or $700,000 dollars, in municipal debt. She would want to shorten maturities, though, changing them from ten years to three to five years at the longest. The reason that she would want to hang on to these is because she needs the income. She would make a change in the allocation of money invested in stocks. This would drop from 30 percent to 10 percent, or $200,000, and cash would increase proportionately from 5 percent to 20 percent, or $400,000. Her 10 percent investment in stock would be her core holdings, or holdings that she has had for quite some time in stable, solid companies like McDonald's, Gillette, Procter and Gamble, Disney, and General Electric. Lauren's account is substantial, but she has much more flexibility than an institution or a mutual fund since they generally have to stay fully invested.

Lauren may want to increase her international stock holdings if our market environment is negative. There is a correlation factor between foreign markets and the U.S. market. Correlation is a mathematical comparison of the relationship of various markets. If the United States is in a negative market, you would want to find international stocks with the lowest correlation to the U.S. market. The premise is that you would want to find stocks with as little in common with the U.S. market as possible so you could make money internationally while waiting for the U.S. market to recover.

Jean's asset allocation will also change in a negative monetary environment. Jean is in a situation different from that of Lauren, because she does not need the income from her investments in order to live. She would get out of treasuries completely. She would hold on to the 25 percent, or $150,000, of her municipal debt instruments that she currently has in her portfolio. Since they are in a laddered portfolio, as one matures she would purchase another. Her stock holdings will drop to 25 percent, and she too will only keep her core holdings. Again, like Lauren, her international holdings may increase during a negative U.S. market. Fifty percent of her money, $250,000, will go into cash or cash equivalents in a negative environment. She also has an advantage over mutual funds or institutional accounts because she can be more flexible and put a high percentage of her money in cash. Mutual funds and institutions rarely have more than 25 percent of their investments in cash.

Terry's situation will remain the same in either market because she is "dollar cost averaging." She is trying to build her holdings and has allocated $200 a month. She will continue to put $150 per month in an index fund (S&P 500) and the other $50 per month in an international fund. Terry is spending the same dollar figure each month but buying fund shares at lower prices.

INTERMARKET OBSERVATIONS

One other tool that should be utilized when determining asset allocation is the futures market or commodities. We are not advocating that you trade futures, merely that you have a working knowledge of them because of their interrelationship to the conventional stock and bond markets. *Most futures traders lose money!*

First let us explain what a futures contract is. When you purchase a stock, you are actually buying a piece of the company. When you buy or sell futures, you are dealing with contracts or arrangements for ownership or sale. A futures contract is an agreement to either buy or sell some commodity—copper, crude oil, cotton, bonds, stocks, etc.—at a specific price and at a specific time in the future. The actual commodity's price, be it cotton, copper, etc., anticipates price movements. The futures contract is a speculation on that anticipation. By studying futures, you can spot extremes in conventional markets and often identify trends that are about to unfold.

To reiterate, all markets are related. Stocks are related to bonds. When copper futures turn up, the stock market turns up. They usually move together and in the same direction. This is because the copper futures are indicating that the economy is gaining strength, and building and industrial projects are increasing. Likewise, if oil futures trend up, bond prices could go down. Remember also that the stock market follows the bond market, so it could also turn down. This occurs because oil is the number one component of raw material prices. It is in almost everything—plastic, fabrics, and carpets, to list just a few examples.

The Commodities Research Bureau Index (CRB Index) is a composite of commodities like the Dow Jones Average is a composite for stocks. If the CRB Index goes up, bonds historically will go down, and the stock market will follow. If the CRB Index goes down dramatically, bond prices will go up, and again the stock market will follow. Alan Greenspan, the chairman of the Federal Reserve, often makes reference to the CRB Index. If the economy is too strong and raw material prices (commodities) rise, he may advise the committee to raise interest rates to slow activity. When interest rates go up or down, it affects all other markets.

Here's an example: the bond market starts to make an extended rise. The stock market follows the bond market. Of the stocks, utilities are usually the first to respond, or go up in this case, because you will remember from our prior discussion that they are interest rate sensitive. Look at a Dow Jones Utility Average chart to spot this trend. The bond futures turn up when investors anticipate a drop in interest rates. Follow the bond futures.

The perception of inflation moves the bond market. The underlying fundamental element of all futures and all markets is supply and demand. There are no other markets that respond to the laws of supply and demand more dramatically than the futures markets. All markets swing to extremes, from extreme overvaluation to extreme undervaluation, because when a market corrects, it tends to overcorrect.

Other interesting trends that can be observed in the futures markets abound. An interesting one is that at the end of the year, large stocks (S&P 500 Index) usually underperform those of the smaller companies (Value Line Index) because the smaller companies often are oversold to an extreme. Investors sell their underperforming stocks before the end of the year in order to take the losses on their taxes.

The smaller companies generally outperform the S&P 500 companies from mid-December through January. This is called the January effect. Knowledge of this phenomenon gives reason to review the long-term relationship of the larger S&P 500 stocks to the broader Value Line Index.

The Value Line Index contains 1,700 stocks, including those that are listed on the S&P 500 along with other smaller companies.

We are not discouraging you from buying small-company stocks. Just be very selective when looking for the extraordinary returns that small stocks can achieve. The returns can be spectacular, especially if you use the principles you learned about choosing individual stocks. Remember to be very demanding—it is your money!

Commodities and the futures market give you a global perspective. It is interesting to familiarize yourself with commodities, futures, and currencies in order to spot trends and because of the interrelationship between all markets. The major futures are charted daily and published in *Investor's Business Daily*. If you have no interest in following futures yourself, at least you now will understand why you will be told that it is mandatory that your broker have a working knowledge of commodities.

This chapter should have pulled together all of the loose ends for you. Next we will look at the important topic of retirement planning, and we will stress the urgency of starting immediately to do some long-term planning. Making money will do you absolutely no good if you do not know how to hold on to it.

Let's summarize.

SUMMARY

- Asset allocation is the distribution of your money among the asset classes in order to achieve your desired investment results.

- There are three asset classes: stocks, bonds, and cash or cash equivalents.
- Look at the monetary environment to determine if it is positive or negative.
- Determine your individual risk tolerance.
- Look at the Risk Line Chart to decide what investments should be held in your portfolio based on your risk tolerance.
- Identify your investment goals.
- Now that you have established the monetary environment, your personal risk tolerance, and your investment goals, remember that allocation strategies should change to adjust to the two different market environments.
- Look at the correlations between the U.S. market and international markets to determine the markets with the lowest correlation to ours—this might be a good money-making possibility in a negative U.S. market.
- Consult with your broker to stay abreast of extremes in the futures market in order to identify trends.

STEP X

AVOIDING THE BIG RISK— OUTLIVING YOUR MONEY

"Cessation of work is not accompanied by cessation of expenses."

— CATO THE ELDER, *DE AGRI CULTURE*

W e call retirement planning "the big risk" or "outliving your money." Imagine that you have been working and saving your entire life, and you have finally accumulated $1 million. You feel you have finally arrived. You have achieved success and financial freedom. *You are a millionaire.* You decide to retire. You are accustomed to living on $100,000 per year, so you continue to spend at that rate. The balance of your money is invested and earning 7 percent interest. Let's assume that inflation is occurring at a rate of 4 percent per year.

You might think that since you are earning 7 percent interest and only have 4 percent inflation, you are in good shape. The truth is that at the end of twelve years you will be penniless.

A recent *New York Times*/CBS poll found that over half of the 1,156 people who were polled were worried about not having enough savings for retirement. Thirty-one percent actually fear that they will personally experience a financial crisis when they retire. This is indeed amazing when you consider that over half of the nonretirees polled had not begun to save or plan for retirement.

People are living longer. If you live to be sixty-five years old, your life expectancy is somewhere between eighty-five and ninety-five years, and one out of five people will live to be ninety-five. You should plan for the ninety-five-year figure and have enough put away to last for the rest of your life.

Most people decide how much to save based on how much they can afford to live without now—not what their long-term retirement income needs are. Financial planners recommend that you put at least 10 percent of your gross income into a retirement savings plan each year. This is a good rule of thumb, but for more accurate information you should fill out "Worksheet 1" on "Retirement: How Much Do You Need?" (Figure 10.1) and "Worksheet 2" on "Budget: How Much Can You Save?" (Figure 10.2).

There are four common errors made in retirement investing:

1. ***Unclear investment objectives.*** You must establish goals, both short and long term.

WORKSHEET 1

RETIREMENT: HOW MUCH DO YOU NEED?

1 Annual retirement income desired. (You'll need roughly 80% of your current
income to maintain your present living standard.)   _____

2 Annual Social Security benefit. (Benefits start at age 62. Enter $11,011 if your
income is $57,600 or more; enter $9,580 if you make $30,000. For a more precise
projection, call Social Security at 800-772-1213.)   _____

3 Annual pension income. (For a rough approximation, multiply your salary by the
number of years service you expect to have at retirement. Then multiply that
result by 0.012. For a more accurate guide, just ask your company's employee
benefits office to estimate your pension in 1994 dollars.)   _____

4 Retirement income needed from savings. (Add line 2 and line 3 and
subtract from line 1.)   _____

5 Future value of additional income needed. (Line 4 times Factor A below.) _____

6 Amount needed at retirement to generate additional income.
(Line 5 times Factor D below.)   _____

7 Future value of what you've already saved. (Total of A, B, & C times Factor B.) _____

A. IRAs, SEPs and Keoghs.	B. Vested amounts in employer plans such as 401(k)s, 403(b)s and profit-sharing accounts.	C. All other investments, including savings accounts, CDs, mutual funds, stocks and bonds.	Factor B

(_____ + _____ + _____) x _____ = _____

8 Total retirement capital you need to accumulate. (Line 6 minus line 7.)   _____

9 Annual savings needed to reach your retirement goal. (Line 8 times Factor C.)   _____

10 What you must save each year until retirement. (Line 9 minus the annual sum
you expect your employer to contribute to your company plan.)   _____

Years to retirement	2	3	4	5	6	8	10	12	14	16	18	20	25	30
Factor A	1.08	1.12	1.17	1.22	1.27	1.37	1.48	1.60	1.73	1.87	2.03	2.19	2.67	3.24
Factor B	1.17	1.26	1.36	1.47	1.59	1.85	2.16	2.52	2.94	3.43	4.00	4.66	6.85	10.06
Factor C	0.481	0.308	0.222	0.170	0.136	0.094	0.069	0.053	0.041	0.033	0.027	0.022	0.014	0.009

Age at Retirement	55	56	57	58	59	60	61	62	63	64	65	66	67
Male Factor D	19.06	18.79	18.52	18.23	17.93	17.62	17.30	16.96	16.62	16.25	15.88	15.49	15.09
Female Factor D	20.03	19.80	19.57	19.32	19.06	18.79	18.52	18.23	17.93	17.62	17.30	16.96	16.62

Source: ICMA Retirement Corporation's *Charting Your Course.*
This was reprinted from the October 1994 issue of *Money* by special permission: Copyright
1994. Time Inc. assumes lifespan for men to be 90 and women, 94. Social Security benefits
estimates assume you stop working at 62. Inflation rate assumed at 4% and return at a
modest 8%, about the historical average for a conservative mix of stocks and bonds.

Figure 10.1

WORKSHEET 2

BUDGET: HOW MUCH CAN YOU SAVE?

		Per Month	Per Year
Your Income	Wages, salary and commissions		
	Dividends, interest and capital gains		
	Annuities, pensions and Social Security (self)		
	Death benefits from estate		
	Income on real property		
	Other		
	Total Income		
Your Expenses	Taxes		
	Mortgage/Rent		
	Food		
	Medical expenses		
	Utilities		
	Telephone		
	Car		
	Clothing		
	Childcare		
	Tuition or education expenses		
	Insurance premiums		
	Maintenance of home		
	Maintenance of car		
	Hobbies		
	Entertainment		
	Vacations		
	Memberships/Professional fees		
	Gifts and donations		
	Loans, credit cards		
	Other		
	Total Expenses		
	Total Income		
	(minus) Total Expenses		
	Total Available for Savings/Investments		

Source: Oppenheimer Funds. "Women and Investing Seminar and Slide Presentation," April 1995.

Figure 10.2

2. *Investing without understanding.* You must make the effort to know and understand what you are buying.

3. *Lack of a clear understanding of tax laws.* You should be familiar with the tax laws that pertain to putting the investments into savings plans and later the tax laws that pertain to taking investments out of the plans.

4. *Ignorance of the time value of money.* Know the true worth of investments where interest or dividends earned are compounded over time. The earning potential can be enormous.

The easiest way to explain retirement planning to you is to equate it to a three-legged stool. In order to have the proper balance, you need all three legs to be in proportion. The first leg is social security. The second leg is your employer's pension plan. Your own retirement planning composes the third leg.

Let's take each of these areas of retirement planning one at a time and examine them. Keep in mind that your retirement income needs to be from 70 to 80 percent of your preretirement income. It is less because you have no working expenses and often your mortgage is paid off at this stage of your life. If you intend to do a lot of traveling in your retirement years, you would want to plan for the higher end of the scale, or aim for the 80 percent figure. If your retirement goals are less costly, you can get by on the 70 percent figure. Try to keep in mind that your retirement career can be longer than your working career. If you are employed from the age of twenty-five and take an early retirement at fifty-five, that equals a thirty-year employment career. If you live to be ninety-five, you will have a forty-year retirement career.

Do you think that you will be able to live solely off your social security benefits? If you answer "no," you have an astute awareness of the problems with social security. In fact, the Social Security Administration's intermediate projection indicates that the annual cash flow will turn negative beginning in 2013 and that the reserve fund will be exhausted in 2029 due to the increase in the elderly population. Even if full benefits are available, keep in mind that the maximum monthly individual benefit payable for a retiree at age sixty-five in 1995 is $1,147. The amount will vary depending on whether benefits continue to be adjusted for inflation and also with your age at retirement. Normal retirement age is now sixty-five but will gradually increase to age sixty-seven by the year 2027. You may elect to receive benefits at age sixty-two but will receive a reduced amount from that point on. To find out the benefit you can expect, call 1-800-772-1213 and ask for a "Request for Earnings and Benefits Estimate Statement."

We have already knocked one leg out from under you, so let's take a look at employer-sponsored pension plans. On average, people change jobs four times in a lifetime. At best, pension plans aim at replacing 40 percent of preretirement income. However, only "lifers" (people who spend their entire career with one company) can expect to collect full benefits.

With the rising costs of health insurance, many employers are eliminating the pension plan from their benefit package, while others are reducing the benefits or converting the plans into 401(k) plans. Of the 1,156 people that the *New York Times*/CBS poll surveyed, nearly half did not have an employer-sponsored pension. Of the employees who do, only 39 percent think it will provide an expected level of benefits at retirement. It is clear to see that if you are only depending on social security and your employer's pension plan for retirement income, you are in serious trouble.

The only leg left is your personal retirement savings plan. You must take responsibility for your own retirement planning. The most logical place to start for the individual is a 401(k) plan. The 401(k) plan replaces the often nonexistent pension plan, so you need to have other savings outside of the 401(k). The sooner you start contributing to a 401(k), the better. This investment is made with pretax dollars, so no income tax is paid on the savings until it is withdrawn. It is automatically withdrawn from your paycheck and is the easiest way to pay yourself first. The maximum contribution is 15 percent of your salary, or $9,500 (in 1995), or whichever comes first. The company will offer you a group of investments that are part of the 401(k) plan, and you can select from these choices. They may be a family of mutual funds, and you can decide between an aggressive growth fund or a balanced fund, for example.

Given this information, it is alarming that only 13 percent of Americans save for retirement by using a 401(k) plan. More than half of all employers will match at least a portion of your 401(k) plan contribution, according to Access Research, a Windsor, Connecticut, consulting firm.

They further cite that of all the people eligible to participate in 401(k) plans, more than one-fourth fail to do so despite the benefits.

Your next question might be, what if I need to get my money out of the 401(k) plan? Generally if you withdraw your money before the age of fifty-nine and one-half, you are penalized and have to pay taxes on the withdrawal as well. Companies usually will not let you withdraw unless you can prove a hardship. Most companies will allow withdrawals without penalty if you are disabled; if you have medical expenses greater than 7.5 percent of your gross income; if the money is going to a divorced spouse under a divorce decree; or, if you die, the law allows your beneficiary to receive the money without paying the penalty.

About 75 percent of companies allow you to borrow half of your vested balance, up to $50,000, according to the consulting firm of Hewitt Associates. You must repay the loan within five years. If you do not, you will owe taxes and the 10 percent penalty. The loan rate is typically one percentage point above prime, but you are paying interest to your own account. You are paying yourself.

We are not advocating that you draw any money out of your 401(k) plan until you are fifty-nine and one-half. In fact, you should invest as much money as possible into it. On April 1, the year after you turn seventy and one-half, you must start to withdraw the money.

Now you understand where the burden of accumulating retirement income will be. If your employer does not offer a 401(k) plan, there are many other options. You should ask your com-

pany's benefits department if any other programs
are available. If no provisions have been made
for retirement planning, perhaps you will be proactive in bringing about a positive change in
your workplace.

Regardless of employer retirement programs,
there are still things an individual can do in addition to the recommended annual investment into
your IRA, or individual retirement account. A variable annuity is another possible option. With a
variable annuity, payments are made into an
account with after-tax dollars. You can put as
much money as you wish as often as you wish into
an annuity that enables you to invest in any of a
thousand mutual funds, and all of the earnings are
completely tax deferred until you retire. As with a
401(k), you are penalized 10 percent for early withdrawal, and also have to pay income taxes on your
earnings upon withdrawal. When you purchase an
annuity, it comes with a life insurance policy that
pays your beneficiary at least the total of all of
your investments if you die before retirement.

There are expenses attached to annuities that
make them less attractive if you think you may
have to withdraw your money early. There are
large fees (up to 9 percent) that are paid to the
insurance company in the form of "surrender
charges" if you withdraw in the early years of the
program. Annuities also charge an annual maintenance fee and annual insurance charges that can
vary depending on your benefits.

If you have invested the maximum allowed in
your pension plans and IRA, an annuity may be a
wise choice for an additional retirement investment. Variable annuities are also useful for retired

people who need to use them as an income vehicle. You can take a systematic withdrawal monthly from an annuity that you already own, or you can purchase one. You could invest the annuity in a high-quality stock mutual fund that is growing at a rate of 10 percent and make monthly withdrawals in the amount of perhaps 7 percent. This converts a growth vehicle into an income vehicle and can add diversification to your portfolio. Too often older people have too heavy a concentration of their portfolio in bonds.

Lauren should have variable annuities as part of her retirement plan for income. Jean should also look at setting up an annuity, because her interest can accumulate tax deferred. Terry is not in a position to need an annuity at the present time, but this is not to say that it is not a good choice for younger clients. It is like a forced savings account.

If you are employed by a smaller company that does not offer a 401(k), it may provide a SEP, or Simplified Employee Pension plan. A SEP is the simplest type of plan. A person who is self-employed with no employees can contribute up to 15 percent or $22,500 for herself annually. If you are self-employed with employees, you can contribute up to 15 percent of your payroll, but the percentage generally must be equal for you and your employees.

Employees do not contribute personally to a SEP program—it is solely employer funded. The money is immediately vested, so the employees can take it out the next day if they want to. All penalties and taxes will apply. A SEP is similar to an IRA in that the employee decides on the investments for herself.

A SAR-SEP, or Salary Deferred Simplified Employee Pension plan, is a variation on a SEP plan. A SAR-SEP has many similarities to a 401(k) in that the maximum one can invest is the lesser of $9,500 or up to 15 percent of the eligible payroll. Your employer can also contribute to the plan for you, but any employer contributions are counted toward the 15 percent limit. This investment is made with pretax dollars, and the tax is deferred until withdrawal. This is also similar to a profit-sharing plan, but there is no seven-year waiting period before you are entitled to the money—it is immediately vested and can be withdrawn at any time. However, there will be penalties of 10 percent on the money if you are less than fifty-nine and one-half, and you will also have to pay ordinary income tax on the withdrawal no matter what your age.

A SAR-SEP has the same maximum deposits, withdrawal penalties, and taxes as a SEP plan, but it has some other restrictions. The place of business cannot have over twenty-five employees, and at least 50 percent of those must participate in the plan. The beauty of this program is that an individual who works for a small company can still have a retirement plan.

Since Jean is a Realtor and thus an independent contractor, she has no company-sponsored pension plan. We would suggest that she start contributing to her own SEP plan now. She can make an annual contribution of 15 percent of her income or up to $22,500, whichever comes first.

There is also another retirement option for Terry, our teacher. Teachers have a plan called a 403(b). There is legislature pending currently to add parity between the 403(b) plan and the 401(k). For the present, let it suffice that Terry should participate up to the maximum allowed for her income level.

Again, the goal is not to make you a retirement specialist, but to make you aware of the need for retirement planning so that you will handle it responsibly. If you need more information on the subject, many good books are available. Another option is to discuss your retirement planning with a CPA, a tax attorney, or an investment advisor who specializes in retirement planning. Just make sure you make the effort to address the subject! Let's summarize.

SUMMARY

- Retirement planning is something that everyone should address as early as possible.
- Decide how much you will need to retire and then budget how much you can save—do not just determine how much you can afford to live without and fail to consider how much you are going to need in your later years.
- There are four common errors made in retirement investing:

  1. Unclear investment objectives.
  2. Investing without understanding.
  3. Lack of clear understanding of tax laws.
  4. Ignorance of the time value of money.

- Retirement planning can be equated to a three-legged stool: Social security, employer pension plans, and individual retirement savings plans make up the three areas. The only real security you have is in your own personal retirement planning, for this is the only area completely under your control.

- Individual retirement plans can include 401(k) plans, SEP plans, 403(b) plans, SAR-SEP programs, annuities, individual investments, and savings, just to mention a few possibilities.

- When setting up a retirement plan, it is advisable to talk to an expert in the field such as a CPA, a tax attorney, or an investment advisor who specializes in retirement planning. Just make sure you have a plan. Something this important should not be left to chance.

Your new knowledge should bring with it a sense of security and well-being—you know how to take care of yourself. There is a glorious feeling of independence that comes along with financial security and well-being. You are probably anxious to try your wings but also a little concerned about falling. In Step XI you will learn your next lesson, how to select a broker. If you feel more comfortable having the help and guidance of a professional investment advisor, knowing how to pick the "right" broker is of utmost importance.

STEP XI

CHOOSING A BROKER

"Everyone knows how, few know when."
— SAM BARTER

C hoosing the right broker is the single most important step you can make in ensuring financial security. For the novice investor, broker selection can be mind boggling. There is a proper method you, the prospective client, should follow to accomplish the procedure of selecting a broker.

The first step is to ask for referrals from friends and family who have similar investment goals. Ask someone whose opinion you trust, such as your attorney or accountant. If you do not know anyone to ask, there are other options available to help you secure a list of qualified brokers to interview. One prospective client called the research department of a major brokerage firm and asked for recommendations of people to pursue. The department recommended a broker who was qualified, did his research, and generally understood the market.

For whatever reason, if these options do not appeal to you, you can always be a "walk-in" client at the brokerage firm of your choice. There are several caution signals to be aware of when using this approach. First, realize that you are going to get the broker du jour. Managers handle rotation differently, but regardless of the criteria used to determine rotation, you are going to get the person who has floor duty that day, experience and qualifications notwithstanding. Participation is at the broker's discretion. Know if you choose this method that you may be dealing with a rookie or someone without a well-developed client base of her or his own. Be prepared to interview several brokers if you choose this approach.

The type of broker and the qualifications that a broker should possess vary, based on your needs and on the amount of money that you have to invest. However, certain facts remain constant and should be examined regardless of individual circumstances. Let us take you through the initial interview.

INTERVIEWING THE BROKER

Do not be intimidated by a fancy office or an expensive suit. You need to find a broker who makes you feel at ease, a person whom you can ask any question that comes to mind. Confidence comes with knowledge. You are the client, and there are basic points that should be discussed at the initial interview. If your prospective broker does not cover all of these points, do not hesitate to thank him for his time and move on to the next interview.

The first section of the interview will be conducted by the broker. He or she will do what interior designers refer to as the programming phase. This is a time for asking questions to learn everything possible about you that will affect your investment portfolio. Again, do not be uneasy about this phase. A good broker will lead you through it.

- The broker is going to ask your age. This is vital for an appropriate investment strategy.

- She or he will need to know your goals. Do you need income from your investments, are you more interested in growth, or do you want a combination of growth and income? Be realistic and do not expect to get rich quick. You should have a long-range investment attitude in order to avoid disappointment and to accomplish long-range financial success.

- Are you saving for retirement, for college for your children, to purchase or improve your home, or for some other goal? It is best to have considered these questions prior to your interview.

- What is the total amount of the assets that you want to invest, your net worth, and your tax bracket?

- What is the approximate time horizon that you wish to invest your money?

- The broker will need to address your tolerance for risk. Everyone is different, and there is volatility and risk in all markets. Examine your attitude toward risk. How much, if any, are you willing to risk? Would you rank yourself as conservative, moderate, or aggressive? Are you interested in a portfolio that incorporates various levels of risk simultaneously? You need to define these terms so that you and the broker have a meeting of the minds. It is mandatory that the broker know exactly what this money means to you. He or she is not there to "sell" to you but rather to solve your problems and to help you accomplish your goals.

- The broker needs to ask you about your job security and if you have a retirement account.

- What are the financial details of your home?

- Are you part of the sandwich generation? The sandwich generation is the group of people who have children at home for whom they are still responsible financially and also aging parents who will become or are already dependent on them. All of these things affect the appropriate investment strategy.

- The broker should also volunteer information about fees, recent or current rates of return, and sales charges on his or her investment recommendations. However, he or she should not be making recommendations on the initial interview. A good broker will be very inquisitive about you and also about the markets. He or she will want to know not only where the markets are but also where they are going and where they have been. The broker should be able to give you an explanation of why he or she is making certain decisions. Very often the decisions the broker is making for you will not be the ones you are reading about in the paper or magazines. The best investments are often the ones that are unpublicized at that time.

If your prospective broker asked you for all of the appropriate information, you will want to make sure that she or he has the proper credentials. The following questionnaire was compiled to determine if a broker has the necessary qualifications that are essential in handling a high-net-worth account. If your account is small and your needs are not complex, you might consider being more lenient in areas such as length of time in business or account size. If your broker can answer all of these questions to your satisfaction (acceptable answers follow the questions) and you feel at ease with her or him, you may have found a nice fit. If not, continue the interview process. You will find the right person. There are many qualified brokers out there.

QUESTIONS AND ANSWERS

Q. How long have you been in business?

A. A broker should have at least five years' experience. You want someone who has seen

enough markets—both upward and downward
trends—and understands both the volatility of
markets and the risks involved. You also do not
want someone who has gotten stale and is no
longer staying on top of the markets. The following questions will help you clarify this.

Q. Would it be unusual for you to handle an
account of *$*? (fill in the amount of money you
intend to invest).

A. If you have $50,000 to invest, you want a
broker who typically deals with accounts in that
range. A broker who customarily handles much
larger accounts may not give you the time and
attention you deserve. By the same token, if the
broker normally handles much smaller accounts,
he or she may not be in tune with the best strategy for your investment.

Q. Ask for a list of satisfied customers
(preferably women) to whom you can speak and
who have similar investment parameters.

A. This is self explanatory. Find out the
client's comfort level with the broker and if she or
he is meeting their expectations.

Q. What is your sell discipline if an investment turns down?

A. You want to hear the broker say that he or
she uses technical analysis to determine buy and
sell points. The broker should use stops to limit
your losses to 10 percent. A "stop" is entered at
the time of purchase. If a stock drops below the

"stop" point, it is automatically sold. This removes the emotion in the decision-making process because the determination of when to sell is made at the time of purchase.

Q. What is your investment philosophy? Do you stay fully invested, or do you use an asset allocation approach?

A. This is a controversial subject. You will make money on the long term if you stay in the stock market and stay fully invested. Stocks, over a long period of time, have proven to be the number-one asset class to own. However, if you are astute enough to get out of a market during bad periods and find alternative investments in other markets, your returns will be higher. Obviously, asset allocation is our recommended approach.

Q. Which charting services do you use?

A. Mansfield Charts (three-year graphs), the Daily Graphs, and Horsey Charts (ten years or longer) are three commonly used charting services. The key to getting a proper perspective is to use a number of different charts that reflect daily activity; intermediate activity, three-year charts; and the long-range picture, ten years or longer.

Q. Do you have a commodities license, and do you follow currencies, interest rates, and financial futures?

A. A commodities license is essential. All brokers should have at least a working knowledge of commodities because commodities are the gateway to all markets. We are not advocating that you trade commodities in your personal account, because most people lose money doing so. A broker who is knowledgeable about currencies, interest rates, and financial futures has an advantage over the uninformed broker. This knowledge can help the informed broker to identify trends in the traditional stock and bond markets.

Q. Do you have a method of defining the client's objectives, a plan to accomplish these objectives, and a means of measuring the progress?

A. Brokers should have a questionnaire to help them define your objectives. They should follow up with a written plan to accomplish these objectives. Once the plan has been implemented, it should be reevaluated at predetermined intervals.

Q. What are a couple of basic investment books that are currently on the market that you have incorporated into your style?

A. Any broker who stays abreast of the markets should readily list two or three good books to help you understand different investment philosophies or the markets in general. We would be especially pleased if he or she mentioned this book!

Q. What sources do you use for independent research outside your brokerage firm?

A. The important point to be made here is that they do independent research. Time and money are required to study outside publications, but doing so broadens a broker's outlook. You do not want a broker who sells you the in-house pick of the week or the product of the month.

Q. Do you have an opinion on the direction of interest rates?

A. The direction of interest rates is a crucial factor in evaluating the markets. When interest rates are declining and money is being put into the system, it creates an excellent environment for stocks. The demand for stocks goes up, since there is money available to buy them. When interest rates are rising, the stock market often turns down, since riskless, fixed-income securities will compete with stocks for the available money.

Q. What are you currently doing in your own account?

A. It is important that the broker know where her or his personal account is year to date and what types of investments she or he has chosen for that account. If the broker does not know the status of her or his own account, that broker certainly will not show any interest in yours. The broker's personal picks can be very revealing, both the selections and the returns on the investments. You will need to know if the broker plans a similar portfolio for you. If not, why? The broker's investment objectives might be different from yours, but you are also going to talk with other women who have objectives similar to yours. Ask them the same questions about rate of return and specific investments.

If your broker passed your test with high marks, there is one more step before you transfer your money. Write or call:

National Association of Securities Dealers

1735 K Street NW
Washington, DC 20006
1-202-728-8000 or
1-800-289-9999

You can find out if the brokerage firm is listed and reputable, and also determine if the broker in question has any complaints on file against him or her. If the broker's record is clean, feel comfortable in knowing that he or she is reputable and knowledgeable. A good broker will put your interests ahead of his or hers. Brokers should guide, counsel, and educate you throughout your investment career, but it is still important to constantly ask questions, trust your instincts, and be an independent thinker.

SUMMARY

- Choosing the right broker and having a sound financial educational foundation are probably the two most important steps you can make in ensuring financial security.
- Ask for referrals of brokers from friends and family who have similar investment goals or someone you trust such as your accountant or attorney. You can also be a "walk-in" client at the firm of your choice.

- The broker will conduct an initial interview to obtain vital information needed to plan your investment portfolio. If the broker is not thorough, or fails to do an adequate interview, move on.

- Ask the prospective broker the questions listed in our questionnaire and make sure that the answers are adequate. If the responses are unacceptable, keep looking.

- Call the National Association of Securities Dealers to check out both the broker and the brokerage firm. You need to know that the broker does not have any complaints on file against him or her and that the brokerage firm is listed and reputable.

Using the Steps
to Take Control
of Your Money

"Investing is about more than money."
—Doug Pi

N ow that you are familiar with the eleven steps to financial independence and security, a brief review may be helpful. It is not enough to just know the information. You need to know how to organize the material so that you can implement it. You learned the information in a logical manner, with each step building on the next. To actually utilize the information, the steps should be considered in a different order; however, developing a focus should still be your first prerequisite.

ACTION ONE: CULTIVATING YOUR FOCUS

Since you began reading this book, if not before, your focus has been directed on becoming financially independent and secure. You are now aware of swings in the economy and should be realizing how the economy impacts you and your family. You are aware of market conditions. Are we in a bull market or a bear market, and what is the Federal Reserve doing to control the demand for money? Is it raising or lowering interest rates? Being aware of these factors will help you develop a new way of thinking that cuts through all of the unnecessary material and allows you to evaluate opportunities in an uncomplicated way. Look for opportunities where no one else is looking. Gather as much information as possible. Listen to everyone but count on yourself. Always try to be selective in the investment process and have the patience to wait for the best opportunities.

One of the most important concepts to remember when developing your focus is to determine your own values and value system. Once you have examined these, do not stray from them. Everyone's priorities are different, but for most they seem to revolve around three general areas: you and your family or loved ones, your faith or your causes and convictions, and your financial security. Once you have established your priorities, you will have a clear focus.

ACTION TWO: ACQUIRING A PLAN

The next step to implement in order to achieve your goal is to consult with a retirement counselor, a financial planning specialist, a CPA, or a tax attorney. This is Step X in the book, entitled "Avoiding the Big Risk—Outliving Your Money." First protect what you have, even if presently it seems like an insignificant amount. Speak with an attorney who specializes in asset protection. Make sure that you have a will. If you do have one, have it reviewed. Circumstances can change so make sure your will protects you in times of serious illness and provides you with the best possible medical care you can afford if you are unable to speak for yourself. Your will and estate plan should enable your loved ones to receive as much as legally possible, tax free, when your assets transfer to them.

We recommend the simplest estate plan—to spend the money enjoying your life. If there is an excess, pass it along to whomever you choose. If you do not protect your money and do short- and long-range financial planning, you will not have anything to invest. Your financial plan does not have to be complicated. We advocate a simple financial plan that will help you to protect you and your family, allow you to contribute to your faith or causes, and help you to establish or maintain financial security. Make sure you have a plan. Something this important should not be left to chance.

Try not to decide how much to save based on what you think you can afford to live without now. Look at your long-term retirement income needs. Financial planners recommend that you pay yourself first. Save at least 10 percent of your gross income each year before paying your bills or spending your money on luxuries.

Avoid the four common errors made in retirement investing:

1. Unclear investment objectives. You must establish goals for both the short and the long term.

2. Investing without understanding. Make the effort to know and understand your investments before making a commitment. If you do not understand the investment, leave it alone.

3. Lack of clear understanding of tax laws. You should be familiar with the tax laws that pertain to putting investments into savings plans and later the tax laws that pertain to taking investments out of the plans.

4. Ignorance of the time value of money. The compounded earning potential can be enormous.

Retirement planning can be equated to a three-legged stool. The first leg is social security. The second leg is your employer's pension plan. Your own retirement planning composes the third leg. It is best to count only on your own retirement savings and plan accordingly. The future of social security is shaky at best, and employer's pension plans are becoming less and less common.

There are many options available for individual retirement planning including 401(k) plans, SEP plans, 403(b) plans, SAR-SEP programs, annuities, individual investments, and savings, just to mention a few. Consult with an expert to establish a personalized investment program that is customized to meet your needs.

ACTION THREE: BE DISCRIMINATING WHEN CHOOSING A FINANCIAL CONSULTANT

Action three is optional. If you feel comfortable enough with the information contained in this book to make all of your investment decisions independently, by all means do so. However, we would advise you to find the "right" financial consultant or broker and use her or his assistance when necessary. There is value added in finding a skilled and experienced financial consultant or broker. If for no other reason, you can better leverage your time by using all of the institution's resources. Professional fees and commissions are a small cost of doing business and are tax deductible in most cases.

If you do choose to use a brokerage firm or bank's financial consultant and you do not already have one whom you know and trust, ask for referrals from friends and family who have similar investment goals or someone you trust such as your accountant or attorney. You can also be a "walk-in" client at the firm of your choice.

Familiarize yourself with the interview process so that you will be able to answer the questions that a broker will ask you. Your financial consultant needs to know everything possible about you that will affect your investment portfolio. If your prospective financial consultant is not thorough or fails to ask the pertinent questions listed in Step XI, move on to your next prospect. Take our questionnaire with you to the interview and ask each question. Make sure that the answers match the ones that follow each question. If the responses are unacceptable, keep looking.

Call the National Association of Securities Dealers at 1-800-289-9999 to investigate the financial consultant and his or her financial institution. Make sure that he or she does not have any complaints on file against him or her and that the brokerage firm is listed and reputable. If all checks out, you are on your way to a relationship that can be very meaningful to you and your family. The true professionals are caring and will act in your best interest. The relationship is worth more than money to them. To a good financial consultant, it is a matter of integrity, knowledge, and hard work for both of you.

Now that you have developed your focus, completed your retirement and financial planning so that you know how much money you can invest, and selected the "right" broker or financial consultant to help you with your investment selections, you are ready to determine your asset allocation.

ACTION FOUR: ALLOCATE YOUR ASSETS

Asset allocation is the single most important decision that you make regarding your investments. Ninety-one and one-half percent of portfolio performance comes from asset allocation. Knowing how to distribute your assets among the three conventional asset classes is paramount to your success in your investment career. The three traditional asset classes are stocks, bonds, and cash or cash equivalents. Stocks are a volatile asset class, bonds are considered to have a moderate risk factor but are subject to interest rate risk and risk of default on income and principal, and cash or cash equivalents are much less volatile with little or no risk. We have simplified asset allocation somewhat by giving you a formula to plug in to determine your investment dispersion. First look at the monetary environment to determine if it is positive or negative. The dominant influence is the monetary environment, or "DIME" as Bill Helman terms it. If the environment is positive, stocks and bonds should both do well. As the environment changes from negative to positive, the bonds should move up first, and the stocks usually follow. At that point, bonds might be a better value relative to stocks. If so, weight your portfolio toward bonds. If the monetary index turns down, we would advise that you raise cash. Some people do not consider cash to be an asset class; however, in a negative market, it is the best conventional asset class to have. At other times commodities or hard assets may outperform cash.

Determine your individual risk tolerance based on the amount or percentage of money you are willing to lose. Do you fall in the low-, medium-, or high-risk category? Once this is determined, you can turn to the Risk Line Chart to find the specific investments that are best for you. You must also consider your personal investment goals. Are you saving for a trip to Europe, or do you need income from your investments to support yourself?

With all of this information in mind, the other tool that you should utilize when determining asset allocation is the interrelationship of markets. All markets are related. If one asset class is affected by changes in interest rates, currencies, commodity prices, supply and demand, the flow of money internationally (think globally), or futures prices, all markets and asset classes will be affected.

It is important to familiarize yourself with commodities and futures to spot trends in the conventional markets. Commodities have a place in everyone's asset mix as a hedge against inflation. Stocks are not a hedge against inflation. In a prolonged bear market for stocks and bonds, good commodity managers usually perform well. Exposure to this asset class should be increased. Commodities are an asset class unto themselves, and major institutional investors are becoming more familiar with them.

Presently institutional investors are under-invested in commodities. This can be an advantage for the individual investor who is a student of the commodities market. No more than 5 to 10 percent of your liquid assets should be committed to this asset class, and professional management is imperative, since most commodity traders lose money. If you have no interest in following futures or commodity prices yourself, at least you understand the necessity for your broker to have at least a working knowledge of them. If you understand all of this information, we feel that it is possible to know when to be in and when to be out of each asset class. If you feel that you are still unclear and do not want to trust this issue entirely to your broker, reread Step IX on Determining Your Asset Allocation.

ACTION FIVE: EMPLOY YOUR FOUNDATION

Once you have determined your proper asset allocation, you need to have a firm foundation on which to build. You must understand the basic theories and terminology of investing. There are only three ways to make money:

1. Earning interest or dividends on the investment.
2. Appreciation of the investment itself.
3. A combination of the two, known as total return.

There are only two types of conventional investments. Investments are either equity (owner) or debt (loaner) investments. Owner investments are stocks, either common stock or preferred stock. When you buy stock, you buy a piece of the company. Historically, of the two, stocks have proven to be the best investment.

The primary reason for buying a stock is capital appreciation. Capital appreciation means that the value of the shares is increasing. When you talk about stock, you are generally referring to common stock. Common stock may or may not pay a dividend. A dividend is the portion of earnings that a company pays out to its stockholders.

Preferred stock is less commonly held. It has reduced risk but also limited returns. Its dividend is paid before the common stock dividend. It is more costly than common stock, but it has a more secure dividend. In the event of bankruptcy, preferred stockholders are paid before common stockholders.

Debt or loaner instruments is the other category. With these investments, you loan your money to someone else, either the U.S. government, a corporation, or a city or municipality, and they pay you interest for the use of your money at a predetermined amount and for a predetermined time period. Debt instruments can be either taxable or nontaxable.

U.S. treasury bills, notes and bonds are taxable on a federal level, but they are exempt from state and local taxes. Taxable debt instruments are U.S. treasury bills, notes, and bonds; zero coupon bonds; government agency bonds; and corporate bonds. Nontaxable instruments are municipal bonds.

Interest rates have a strong relationship to bonds. If interest rates go up, the value of bonds will go down. If interest rates go down, the value of bonds goes up. This is a very important concept because the direction of interest rates will affect when or if you purchase bonds and will affect the other asset classes as well.

It is also important to remember that the big money will flow to the investments with the least risk and the highest return. Pay attention to what large investors are doing and try to stay one or two steps ahead of them. Look to where the demand may be going. The average investor only looks where demand is obvious.

Now that your investment foundation is firmly established, let's review the taxable bond market in more depth.

ACTION SIX: LEND MONEY TO YOUR GOVERNMENT

The taxable income market is composed of U.S. treasury bills, notes, and bonds; zero coupon bonds; government agency bonds; and corporate debt. Always look at the thirty-year U.S. treasury bond, or "long bond," and weigh all investments against it, because the treasury bond is considered to be a low-risk investment since it is backed by the U.S. government. It is also a good idea to be even more cautious and to compare everything to the investment that is presumed to have the lowest risk—the treasury bill.

The market for U.S. debt instruments is the largest and most actively traded in the world. It is an extremely liquid market. Liquidity is the ability of an instrument to be bought or sold quickly in various amounts without disturbing the price substantially. You can sell treasuries, and the money, or the principal and interest, must be in your account by the next day.

There are three strong forces that drive the bond market. The first is the natural market force of supply and demand. The second strong force that moves the bond market is the Federal Reserve, which raises or lowers interest rates to control the demand for money and thus controls the monetary environment. Your fellow investors' perceptions of inflation, correct or incorrect, is the third strong force that affects the bond market.

There are two common bond strategies that you need to examine, laddered portfolios and actively managed portfolios for total return, but first remember the ten-year rule. Do not commit your money for a period longer than ten years. Every investor wants to make the most money for the least amount of risk, and history has proven that intermediate-term investments (with treasuries, that is, two to ten years) have provided 85 percent of the income that long bonds provide with less risk due to the shorter maturity. The two-year note is one of the best grazing spots for cash that will be committed to other assets in the near future.

The laddered portfolio strategy uses staggering maturities, so that you have a treasury issue maturing every year for ten years. As one instrument matures, you would purchase another maturing in ten years. It is an effective strategy for treasuries, corporates, and municipal debt.

Actively managed portfolios for total return strategy require constant attention. Leave this strategy to the discretion of a professional manager, as adjustments are made whenever a market starts to fluctuate. This strategy is used both to acquire capital appreciation and to earn interest that is reinvested. This is total return.

Zero coupon bonds are sold at a discounted amount like treasury bills. The term of maturity is ten years or longer. Zero coupon bonds are backed by the U.S. government, but they are issued by brokerage firms, corporations, and municipalities. They are often used to fund college educations or retirement plans because the purchaser can pick the date of maturity. These bonds are susceptible to volatile price swings if sold before maturity.

Government agency bonds were formed to promote housing and farming, and they are rarely purchased by an individual. They may be a part of a mutual fund portfolio. The selection of these should be left to a government agency bond specialist.

Most investors should avoid corporate debt. Selections should be left to the professionals. The interest rate spread between corporate debt and treasuries is usually small and not worth the additional risk. Corporate debt instruments perform better than treasuries in a robust economy. Corporate debt as well as municipal and government agency debt instruments are all rated. U.S. treasuries are not rated, but they are the highest quality of all.

Our next topic to examine and review is tax-free instruments or municipal bonds.

ACTION SEVEN: LOWER YOUR TAXES AND HELP YOUR NEIGHBORHOOD

Municipal debt is sold by states, cities, or other local governments, usually to finance the building of roads, schools, bridges, or hospitals. Municipal debt can be short-term notes, intermediate-term notes, or longer term bonds with maturities ranging from one month to forty years. It is usually sold in $5,000 increments.

Municipal debt is exempt from federal taxes and can be exempt from state and local taxes if you purchase the issue from the state and municipality in which you reside. Since interest is exempt from federal tax, the amount of interest, or the yield, will be lower than that for treasury or corporate debt of equal maturity. You should always consider the after-tax yield, or the actual amount of income you keep after taxes are deducted from treasuries and corporates (as everyone's tax bracket is different), and then compare that figure to the return on a municipal in order to make a sound comparison. Commissions are included in the price of a bond, so ask what you are paying when you are buying and selling.

The two most common types of municipal bonds are general obligation bonds (GOs) and revenue bonds. General obligation bonds are backed by the full faith and taxing power of the issuer and are more secure than revenue bonds. Revenue bonds are backed by a specific revenue source instead of the full taxing power of the municipality. For example, a hospital will back its own revenue bond.

Short-term municipal debt instruments have maturities ranging from three months to three years and could fit very nicely into an individual's portfolio. There are seven companies that insure municipal debt based on its soundness and ratings. Most people should only buy AAA-rated, insured issues or prerefunded bonds. A prerefunded bond is escrowed with U.S. treasuries before its call date arrives so that the municipality can remove it from its books and sell more bonds. When a bond is prerefunded, the call date becomes the maturity date, the rating becomes AAA, and the bond trades at lower yields.

After you have examined the possibilities of investing in taxable and tax-free debt instruments, you will need to look at stocks or equity investments.

ACTION EIGHT: DISCERNING THE RHETORIC OF COMMON STOCK

The key thing to remember when dealing with any investment, especially stocks, is to make sure that you understand the investment. If you do not understand, ask questions and reread the chapters on stock. If you still do not understand, pass on stocks and invest in things that you do understand.

Before you can pick individual stocks, you need to be familiar with the categories of stock that are available. Stocks are equity or owner instruments because the purchaser is actually buying a piece of a company. Historically, stocks have proven to be the best conventional asset class to own. The expected return from being fully invested in stocks is around 10 percent—in the past, approximately 4 percent of that came from dividends and 6 percent came from price appreciation. However, if you look at recent returns, the market has not met that expectation. Our recommendation is that you buy large-cap stocks in solid companies. Conventional wisdom is that you should buy small-cap stocks; they are the most volatile, but by far the preferred asset class for appreciation and return. Our research did not bear this out; however, if you are capable of picking small companies, this is where the big money is made.

There are four basic categories of stock: growth stock, cyclical stock, defensive stock, and American depository receipts (ADRs).

There are three kinds of growth stocks: large-capitalization or cap, mid-cap, and small-cap. Capitalization is the price of the stock times the amount of shares outstanding.

Large-cap growth stocks are stocks of large, mature companies. They have moderate risk and often have moderate returns, but growth is steady in all economic cycles. However, high-quality stocks can have periods where they outperform the smaller, more volatile stocks. They normally reinvest the profits or earnings of the company instead of paying a high dividend. Examples are Gillette, Coca-Cola, and Disney.

Mid-cap growth stocks are stocks from medium-sized companies with slightly more risk than large-cap growth companies, but there is also the possibility of higher returns. This is especially true when the U.S. dollar is strong. Examples are The Limited and Pier One Imports.

Small-cap growth stocks are stocks from the youngest, fastest growing companies. They offer the highest risk and can be volatile but also provide the possibility of the highest returns. Examples are Fastenal and CUC International.

Cyclical stocks are sensitive to economic cycles. By now you should be able to identify economic cycles. Always try to invest a stage ahead of the crowd and wait for them to catch up. The earnings per share can vary, based on the strength or weakness in the economy. This makes their earnings more volatile. They may pay higher quarterly dividends to the stockholders instead of reinvesting the profits into the company. There are three types: large-cap cyclical, mid-cap cyclical, and small-cap cyclical.

Large-cap cyclical stocks are stocks from big, mature companies that are sensitive to the economic cycles. They offer moderate risk and moderate return. General Motors is a good example of a large-cap cyclical.

Mid-cap cyclicals are stocks of moderate-sized companies that have a higher risk and higher return potential than large-cap cyclical. The Ryland Group is an example.

Small-cap cyclicals are stocks from smaller companies that provide the highest risk and the highest return. Sterling Electronics is a good example.

Defensive stocks are the third category. Buy these when you think interest rates have peaked, but remember that it takes approximately six months for the Federal Reserve activity to be reflected in the market. Defensive stocks are stocks that do well in a slow economic environment. Utility stocks are an example of defensive stocks. Utilities offer a high yield and are generally purchased for the dividend. Other examples are food stocks and soaps.

American depository receipts (ADRs) are the fourth category. American depository receipts are certificates that represent ownership of foreign shares that are held abroad by U.S. banks located in a foreign country. They are subject to currency fluctuations and can be either growth or cyclical. Follow global interest rates and currency trends and place your money where you think the crowd is going, not where they are now. Both the dividend and capital appreciation are paid in U.S. dollars. Sony and Toyota are examples.

Another concept that deserves review is value investing. Value investing is investing in companies that are perceived to be unloved and out of favor so that you can buy low and sell higher. The following are three examples of value investing: *turnarounds* are companies that are restructuring debt or management or both, *asset plays* involve undervalued assets on the books of a corporation such as oil and gas or real estate that it has been holding for many years or overfunded pension plans that one can take advantage of by buying low, and *special situations* involve buying for a specific purpose for a specific expected result and fundamental change such as a takeover.

Inside information is useless. If you have it, do not use it. If you do not have it, do not invest in rumor stocks. During the 1980s many investors had inside information, and they are now outsiders on Wall Street. Value investing can involve either growth or cyclical stocks.

Blue chip stocks can be an ambiguous term. They can be either growth or cyclical. They are stocks from the biggest companies such as the thirty Dow Jones Industrial stocks, but they can go down in value and are not without risk.

A top-down approach for buying and selling stocks involves deciding on the current economic stage—either a recession, early stage recovery, late stage recovery, or expansion—then determining which groups of stocks to own based on the current economic stage.

After you feel completely comfortable with this information, it is time to move on to how to pick individual stocks.

ACTION NINE: SELECTING SUBSTANTIAL STOCKS

Before you select an individual stock, you should first use a top-down approach. You should examine the monetary environment, interest rates, and the economy. Your second step is to investigate market psychology. The third element to consider is valuations. Valuations determine whether the market is historically high or low. Once you have done this, you are ready to examine stocks through the two basic disciplines—technical and fundamental analysis. Always use both disciplines, but start your evaluation with technical analysis.

Before moving to individual stocks, you should first review industry groups through technical analysis to determine areas of strength. Next, review technical patterns of individual stocks within the groups. Pick the strongest company in the strongest industry. Look for groups that are about to emerge.

Technical analysis charts are pictures of supply and demand of particular stocks over a certain amount of time. The patterns can be clearly bullish or bearish. The resistance is the selling pressure or the overhead supply. Support is buying pressure that occurs when buyers come in and keep a stock from falling lower. Breakout occurs when the stock has broken through the selling pressure or resistance and moves higher.

Always look at three different time spans when using technical analysis—long term (ten years or longer), intermediate (three year), and short term (one year) charts. Technical analysis can help you determine where to put your stops when you purchase a stock, so you can cut your losses short and let your profits run.

After using technical analysis to isolate individual stocks, look at the fundamentals of each company. Do this only after the technicals point to a specific investment. With fundamental analysis, you examine a company hoping to find a high return on equity, a low percentage of debt, high net cash flows, high-quality management of the company, and a high ratio of current assets versus current liabilities. High profitability with fewer assets is usually positive since there is less money going into the maintenance of those assets.

Look for companies that make a high margin of profit and can distinguish themselves from the competition. Seek out companies that provide value to the end user, have integrity, and have a high level of enthusiasm and productivity and companies where the lowest employee on the pay scale both acts and feels like an owner. American Express and Disney are two good examples. Lastly, become comfortable with the concept that you have to pay for quality.

This brings us to the point where we need to address money managers.

ACTION TEN: SCRUTINIZING MONEY MANAGERS

There are circumstances where money managers can serve a purpose in your investment career, but for the most part a rare few add value. Money managers are investment advisors with highly specialized styles and investment philosophies. There are two conventional categories of money managers—fixed-income or bond managers and equity or stock managers. Fixed-income managers are either taxable or nontaxable managers. Some taxable managers add value to your account, but we do not recommend tax-free managers except for some high-quality mutual fund managers. There are six types of equity managers: value managers, growth managers, sector rotation managers, asset allocation managers, balanced managers, and international managers. Of all the types of equity managers, we would recommend asset allocation managers and international managers and a select few balanced managers.

When using a money manager, the client owns individual stocks and bonds, not shares in a pooled account. Fees are prorated, and the wrap fee is the most commonly used. There is no penalty for closing out an account. Accounts must be $100,000 or more. If you want to use a manager, you should work with your financial consultant to select a manager who best suits your goals and risk tolerance and to advise you on the right type of manager.

This brings us to our final point of action—mutual funds.

ACTION ELEVEN: CULLING MUTUAL FUNDS

Mutual funds are investments that pool your money with that of other investors. Know your goals and pick your target based on them, not on a net cost basis only. Consider this six-point checklist before buying a mutual fund:

1. What percentage of your total assets are going into the fund?
2. How long are you going to hold the fund?
3. Do you have a particular goal for these funds?
4. Do you need income from this money?
5. What volatility are you willing to accept over your chosen time horizon?
6. Examine the cost structure based on the time period that you plan to hold the funds.

Open-end mutual funds are the most common. The number of shares is directly proportional to the amount of money going into or out of the fund. There are four conventional types of open-end mutual funds: money market funds, bond funds, balanced funds, and stock funds. Funds invested in bonds can be either taxable or tax free. Know why you are purchasing the fund and what you hope to accomplish. There are six types of stock funds depending on the type of stocks that are held within a fund: growth funds, value funds, index funds, sector funds, global funds, and international funds. There are also some excellent commodity funds with limited risks for the average investor. They can be purchased in your IRA or retirement account if you meet suitability requirements. A $2,000 minimum investment for retirement accounts is not uncommon.

Closed-end funds are not as common. They issue shares one time and then trade on a major stock exchange just like an individual stock.

Examine risk versus reward before buying any mutual fund. Know the fees and sales loads you are going to pay before you purchase any fund. These will affect your return. Remember that it is often possible to switch a fund within the same family of funds without paying additional fees or commissions. Do not select a mutual fund because it had one good year. Look long term and compare the returns. Do your homework!

If you heed these simple cautions, there may be a place in your portfolio for some type of mutual fund. Do not invest with a rearview mirror. Last year's "hot fund" may very well be this year's loser.

We have covered a vast amount of material in this book, building a solid foundation of investment principles and instruments, and we have shown you the order in which you should implement them to best profit by the information. It is our hope that you meet with success in your investment ventures, that you persevere to hone your investment skills, and that you continue to be a student of the markets.

GLOSSARY

A shares are front-end loads on mutual funds. With this type of sales load you pay the costs up front. You should stay in this type of fund for six years or longer.

Actively managed portfolios for total return bond strategy should be left to the discretion of a professional manager. When a market starts to fluctuate, adjustments are made.

American Depository Receipts (ADRs) are certificates that represent ownership of foreign shares that are held abroad by United States banks located in a foreign country. They are subject to currency fluctuations and can be either growth or cyclical. The investor in an ADR receives both the dividend and the capital appreciation in U. S. dollars.

Asset allocation managers make bold portfolio movements. They can be one hundred percent invested in stock or one hundred percent invested in cash if they feel the market is vulnerable. Considered to be for more conservative investors, these managers will attempt to go to cash in a down market so you will not lose your money; however, in an up market they will make less.

Asset plays involve undervalued assets on the books of a corporation. The idea is to take advantage of these undervalued items and buy low. This is an example of value investing.

B shares are back-end loads on mutual funds. When using this structure, you pay a deferred load when you sell the fund. It is a declining back-end load, which means the longer you hold the fund, the less of a sales load you will have to pay. Twelve B-1 fees are charged annually on back-end load funds.

Balanced managers manage stocks and bonds in the same portfolio.

Bear market is a downward-trending market.

Blue chip stocks can be growth or cyclical. They are "perceived" to be the least risky. They are the biggest companies. The thirty Dow Jones Industrial stocks are in this category. A blue chip stock can go down in value—it is not a guarantee of safety.

Book value is the assumed valuation of a company if it were liquidated—all assets minus all liabilities, divided by the number of shares outstanding.

Bull market is an upward-trending market.

C shares on mutual funds have no front-end loads, but they do have a higher management fee. If you plan to hold the fund for five years or more, a front-end load may be better.

Capitalization is the price of the stock times the amount of shares outstanding.

Closed-end mutual fund shares are issued just one time, and are then traded on a major exchange like the New York Stock Exchange, just like an individual stock.

Commodities Research Bureau Index (CRB Index) is a composite of commodities like the Dow Jones Average is a composite for stocks.

Corporate bonds are loans to a corporation. These bonds are rated according to the credit-worthiness of the issuer. The higher the credit rating of the corporation, the less interest they pay to the bond holder. Maturities can be short-, intermediate-, or long-term. The minimum investment is $1,000.

Cyclical stocks are sensitive to economic cycles. The earnings per share can vary based on the strength or weakness in the economy. Cyclical stocks may pay higher quarterly dividends to stockholders instead of reinvesting the profits into the company. There are three types of cyclical stocks: large-cap, mid-cap, and small-cap.

Debt or loaner investments are investments where you loan your money to someone else, either the U. S. government, a corporation, or a city, and are paid interest for the use of your money at a predetermined amount and for a predetermined time period. They are either taxable or non-taxable.

Defensive stocks are stocks that do well in a slow economic environment. Examples are food, soap, and utility stocks. These are companies that make products people need, even in a recession.

Discount rate is the rate the Federal Reserve charges banks to borrow money.

Dow Jones Utility Average is an index of utility stocks.

Equity investments or owner investments are stock investments, either common or preferred. When you buy a stock you buy a piece of the company.

401(k) plan is an individual retirement plan made with pre-tax dollars, so no income tax is paid on the savings until it is withdrawn. The maximum contribution is 15 percent of your salary or $9,240 per year, whichever comes first.

Fundamental analysis considers the industry evaluations of a particular stock and then looks at earnings growth rate, price-to-earnings ratio, return on equity, the management of a company, and its dividends, and compares the current assets versus the current liabilities. Look at these factors after technical analysis has pointed toward a specific stock.

General obligation bonds (GOs) are a common type of municipal bond. They are backed by the full faith and taxing power of the issuer or, in other words, the issuer will raise taxes without limit to repay you.

Government agency bonds are issued by mortgage associations and backed by government agencies but are not a direct obligation of the U. S. government. They are AAA-rated. Ginnie Mae, Fannie Mae, and Freddie Mac are the three most well known.

Growth managers invest exclusively in growth stocks.

Growth stock has a steadily growing earning stream—regardless of the economic environment. Growth stocks generally have a higher price-to-earnings ratio. These can be large-cap, mid-cap, or small-cap growth stocks. They normally reinvest the profits or earnings of the company instead of paying a high dividend.

Ibbotson charts plot the historic return on treasury bills, treasury bonds, large-cap stocks found in the S&P 500, small-cap stocks, and inflation. It generally goes back to 1926.

International managers invest primarily in American depository receipts (ADRs) of foreign corporations. They can be either value or growth style managers.

Laddered portfolio is an effective bond strategy that uses staggering maturities so that one has a bond maturing every year for ten years. Every year, as one instrument matures, you would purchase another maturing in ten years.

Monetary Pressure Index determines the market environment for both stocks and bonds.

Money managers are investment advisors with highly specialized styles and investment philosophies. They fashion their styles after a particular stock or bond class. Managers are either fixed income managers (bonds) or equity managers (stock) or combinations of the two (balanced).

Municipal bonds are sold by states, cities, and other local governments. They are traded in $5,000 increments. Maturities range from one month to forty years.

Municipal notes have a maturity ranging from three months to three years and are issued to raise money for temporary financing of capital improvements or to even out cash flows of municipalities.

Mutual funds are investments that pool your money with the money of other investors.

NAV is the net asset value per share. The NAV is the value of one share in a mutual fund, which fluctuates daily.

No-load mutual funds do not charge sales loads but have management fees.

Open-end mutual funds issue shares on a continuing basis. The number of shares increases as money comes into the fund and decreases as shares are redeemed.

Prerefunded bonds are callable, but at some time before the call date arrives the municipality backs the bonds with U.S. treasuries. A city or municipality has a limit to the amount of debt it can have on its books, so when a municipality pre-refunds a bond, this removes the bond from the books and enables the municipality to sell more bonds. When a bond is pre-refunded, the call date becomes the maturity date and the rating becomes AAA. These are the safest form of municipal investments.

Price-to-earnings ratio is the ratio that is derived from dividing the price of the stock by the annual earnings per share.

Revenue bonds are another type of municipal bond. They are backed by a specific revenue source instead of the full taxing power of the municipality.

SAR-SEP or salary deferred simplified employee pension plan is a variation on a SEP plan. The maximum investment is $9,240 per year or up to 15 percent of the eligible payroll. Employers may contribute to the plan, but these contributions are counted toward the 15 percent limit. This investment is made with pre-tax dollars and is tax deferred until withdrawal.

Sector rotation managers do less stock picking. They are more concerned with being in the right industry at the right time.

SEP, or simplified employee pension plan, is for a person who is self-employed with no employees or self-employed with employees. Employees do not contribute personally to a SEP program—it is solely employer funded.

Special situation is buying for a specific, expected result and fundamental change such as a takeover. This is an example of value investing.

Stop loss is the point where you want to sell your stock. It can be entered at the time of purchase. If your stock drops to your "stop," it will automatically be sold. Stops remove the emotion involved in selling stock.

Technical analysis is a chart of a stock's performance based on supply and demand.

Top-down approach is the preferred approach for buying and selling stocks. One first examines the economy to determine its stage—whether it is in a recession, early stage recovery, late stage recovery, or expansion. Next look at stocks that do well in the current stage.

Turnaround refers to a company that is restructuring debt or restructuring management, or restructuring both debt and management. This stock is considered value investing.

U. S. treasury bills are a loaner investment. When you buy a U.S. treasury bill you are lending money to the government. It is the lowest risk investment available, and it is backed by the U.S. government. Treasury bills are purchased at a discounted rate and at maturity are worth the face value. Minimum purchase is $10,000. "T-bills" will have a three-month, six-month, or one-year maturity.

U. S. treasury bonds are long-term investments or loans to the U.S. government. Maturities are ten years or longer. One thousand dollars is the minimum purchase.

U. S. treasury notes are a loan to the U.S. government. A treasury note is an intermediate term security with a two- to ten-year maturity. The minimum investment is $1,000 and interest is paid semiannually.

Valuations determine whether the market is historically high or low. Look at price-to-dividend ratios, price-to-earnings ratios, and price-to-book values.

Value investing is investing in companies in order to buy low and sell higher, because those companies are perceived to be unloved or out of favor.

Value managers invest in stocks they consider to be undervalued.

Yield curve is the variation in return between short-, intermediate-, and long-term investments. One tries to get the highest yield with the least amount of fluctuation.

Zero coupon bonds are instruments that are sold at a discounted amount like a treasury bill. They are highly susceptible to interest rate swings if sold before maturity. They are often used to fund college educations or retirement funds, because one can select the actual date of maturity when she purchases the bond and know the exact amount of the yield.

SOURCES CONSULTED

Belsky, Gary. "The Five Ways Women Are Often Smarter than Men about Money." *Money* (June 1992): 74–78, 80–82.

Belsky, Gary. "What Women Really Want." *Money* (June 1992): 79.

Belsky, Gary, and Beth Kobliner. "He Says, She Says: How Men and Women Differ about Money." *Money* (November 1993): 76–84.

Boone, Louis E. *Quotable Business*. New York: Random House, 1992.

Carey, Mary-Lee, retirement plan director at a major brokerage firm. Personal interview.

Chilton, David. *The Wealthy Barber*. Rocklin, California: Prima, 1993.

Clason, George S. *The Richest Man in Babylon*. New York: Plume, 1955.

Dalton, John M., ed. *How the Stock Market Works*. New York: New York Institute of Finance (NYIF, a division of Simon and Schuster), 1993.

Dugas, Christine. "Fiscal Fitness, Opportunity Knocks." *Newsday,* 2 January 1994.

Edwards, Robert D., and John Magee. *Technical Analysis of Stock Trends*. 6th ed. New York: New York Institute of Finance (NYIF), 1992.

Emerson, Henry. "Lecture by Charles T. Munger to the students of Professor Guilford Babcock at the University of Southern California, School of Business." *Outstanding Investor Digest*, 5 May 1995, 49–63.

Goldstein, Sharon. *The Merriam-Webster Dictionary of Quotations*. Springfield, Massachusetts: Merriam-Webster, 1992.

Graham, Benjamin. *The Intelligent Investor*. New York: Harper & Row, 1973.

Graham, Benjamin, and David L. Dodd. *Security Analysis*. 4th ed. New York: McGraw-Hill, 1962.

Greene, Katherine, and Richard Greene. "Is Financial Advice Sexist?" *Working Woman* (September 1993): 56–59, 104.

Hagstrom, Robert G., Jr. *The Warren Buffett Way*. New York: John Wiley & Sons, 1994.

Hill, Napoleon. *Think and Grow Rich*. New York: Ballantine Books, 1960.

Little, Jeffrey B., and Lucien Rhodes. *Understanding Wall Street*. United States: Liberty Hall Press (an imprint of McGraw-Hill), 1991.

Lynch, Peter. *One Up on Wall Street*. New York: Penguin Books, 1990.

Lynch, Peter. *Beating the Street*. New York: Simon and Schuster, 1994.

Montgomery, Anthony. "No-Loaders Don't Tell Whole Truth." *Financial Planning on Wall Street* (May 1994): 51–52.

Morris, Kenneth M., and Alan M. Siegel. *Guide to Understanding Money and Investing*. New York: Lightbulb Press, 1993.

Murphy, John. "Using Bar Charts to Forecast Meat Futures Prices." *Trading Futures, a Livestock Futures Anthology*. Chicago: Chicago Mercantile Exchange, 1986, 65–81.

Murphy, John J. *Intermarket Technical Analysis*. New York: John Wiley & Sons, 1991.

O'Neil, William J. *How to Make Money in Stocks*. New York: McGraw-Hill, 1988.

Oppenheimer Funds. "Women and Investing Seminar and Slide Presentation," April 1995.

Registered Representative Series 7 Study Program. Vols. 1 and 2. Greenwich, Connecticut: Edward Fleur Financial Education Corporation, 1993.

Reid, Victoria. "How to Learn about Money Management." *Florida Today*, 16 May 1994, 6E.

Reid, Victoria. "Taking Care of Business." *Florida Today*, 16 May 1994, 6E.

Reid, Victoria. "Women Are Working More, Earning Less." *Florida Today*, 16 May 1994, 6E.

Robbins, Lynn G., with Dennis Webb and Lisa Vermillon. *Uncommon Cents*. Salt Lake City, Utah: Franklin International Institute, 1989.

Schwarz, Jordan A. *The Speculator, Bernard M. Baruch in Washington 1917–1965*. Chapel Hill: University of North Carolina Press, 1981.

Sease, Douglas, and John Prestbo. *Barron's National Business and Financial Weekly Guide to Making Investment Decisions*. New Jersey: Prentice Hall, 1994.

Shaw, Alan R. *Technical Analysis*. 2nd ed. Burr Ridge, Illinois: Irwin Professional Publishing, 1988. Reprinted from *Financial Analyst's Handbook*, 2nd Edition, edited by Sumner L. Levine.

Shearson Lehman Brothers. "Four Common Errors of Retirement Investing." *Plan Perspectives* (fourth quarter 1992): 3.

Shearson Lehman Brothers. "Plan Now for a Financially Secure Retirement." *Plan Perspectives* (fourth quarter 1992): 1, 4.

Shearson Lehman Brothers. "Are You Saving Enough for Retirement?" *Plan Perspectives* (third quarter 1993): 1, 2.

Smith Barney. *Plan Perspectives* (third quarter 1995): 1, 2.

Sorros, George. *The Alchemy of Finance.* New York: John Wiley & Sons, Inc., 1987.

Stanley, Thomas J. *Selling to the Affluent.* Homewood, Illinois: Business One Irwin, 1991.

Thompson, Terri. "Your Money-Investment Clubs: Women Do Best." *Working Woman* (September 1991): 50.

Waggoner, John. "Contribute to Your 401(k) 'Until It Hurts': Dipping into Funds Early Carries Price." *USA Today*, 20 February 1995, 48.

Wall, Ginita, CPA, CFA. "Understanding Women Investors." *Registered Representative* (February 1994): 58, 60, 63–64.

Wang, Penelope. "Brokers Still Treat Men Better than Women." *Money* (June 1994): 108–110.

Weinstein, Grace W. "Gearing Up for a Secure Future." *Barron's*, 19 September 1994, 34.

Weinstein, Stan. *Secrets for Profiting in Bull and Bear Markets.* Burr Ridge, Illinois: Irwin Professional Publishing, 1988.

Zayacheck, Jon. *Jon Z's Primer.* New Jersey: X-Rho Enterprises, 1988.

Zweig, Martin. *Winning on Wall Street.* New York: Warner Books, 1994.

INDEX

213

sensitivity of, 143
technical strength of, 78

V

Valuations, 76
  defined, 205
Value funds, 123, 194
Value investing, 66–67, 190
  defined, 205
Value Line Index, 59, 89–90
  high-quality mature
    companies and, 103
  January effect, 143–144
  small-cap growth stock
    funds, 122
Value managers, 102, 193
  defined, 205
Variable annuities, 155–156
Volatility of mutual fund, 115

W

Waiver of fees, 127
Walk-in clients, 162
The Wall Street Journal, 85
Wall Street Week, 8

Walmart, 92
Walt Disney Company. *See*
  Disney
Walton, Sam, 92
The Warren Buffett Way
  (Hagstrom), 91
Wealth indices of
  investments, 59
Weinstein, Stan, 91
Wrap fees, 107

Y

Yield curves, 23
  defined, 205

Z

Zacks, 91
Zero coupon bonds, 23,
  41–42, 183
  defined, 205
  discounted amount, sale
    at, 184
  maturity of, 41
  taxes on, 42

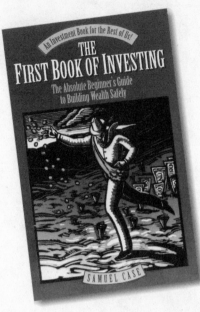

The First Book of Investing

Samuel Case

This easy-to-understand guide for beginners covers everything from stocks, bonds, and real estate to rare coins and futures contracts. Each chapter begins with an explanation of the basics: WHAT stocks and bonds are, WHY investors want to buy them, and HOW to buy them. Only then does the author describe more advanced concepts, such as the best way to invest.

The Tao of Money

Ivan Hoffman

Money is one of the most emotional issues today. Ivan Hoffman shows us that our personal financial harmony is worldwide financial harmony. The way we perceive money has a direct impact on our ability to translate that harmony into worldwide issues.

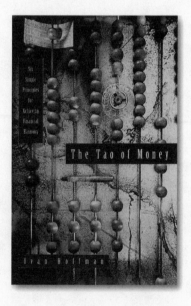

The Socially Responsible Guide to Smart Investing

Samuel Case

A cleaner, healthier planet. Humanitarian employment practices. Drug and smoke-free environments. Alternative energy sources. Higher goals like these don't have to rule our higher corporate profits. In fact, some of the best ideas for improving the world are also the most successful new business opportunities! Sam Case reveals how to optimize the return on investments without abandoning or ignoring one's conscience.

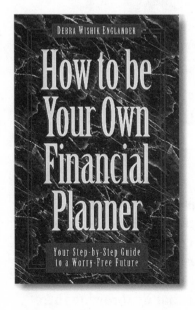

How to Be Your Own Financial Planner

Debra Wishik Englander

For those who already use a planner, broker, insurance agent, or other professional, this book will ensure that they are getting their money's worth from the experts. For the novice who can barely balance a checkbook, this book provides the basics of budgeting and how to make money not only last longer, but earn more.

The Wealthy Barber,
Updated 2nd Edition

David Chilton

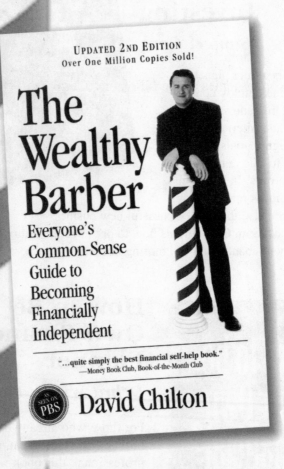

The Wealthy Barber is a fastpaced story set in Hometown, USA. Roy, a quiet wealthy small-town barber, combines simple concepts, common sense, and an insight into human nature to reshape the shaggy financial affairs of his barbershop patrons. He does this not by badgering them about budgeting, but by throwing them practical, easy-to-implement guidelines that anyone can use.

FILL IN AND MAIL TODAY

PRIMA PUBLISHING
P.O. Box 1260BK
Rocklin, CA 95677

USE YOUR VISA/MC AND ORDER BY PHONE
(916) 632-4400
Monday—Friday 9 A.M.—4 P.M. PST

I'd like to order copies of the following titles:

Quantity	Title	Amount
_____	*The First Book of Investing*	$14.95
_____	*How to Be Your Own Financial Planner*	$20.95
_____	*Socially Responsible Guide to Smart Investing*	$19.95
_____	*The Tao of Money*	$10.95
_____	*The Wealthy Barber, Updated 2nd Edition*	$12.95

Subtotal_____

Postage & Handling ($3 for first book,

$1 for additional books)_____

7.25% Sales Tax (California only)_____

TOTAL (U.S. funds only)_____

Check enclosed for $_____ (payable to Prima Publishing)

Charge my   ❏ MasterCard   ❏ Visa

Account No. _____

Exp. Date_____

Signature

_____

Your Name

_____

Address

_____

City/State/Zip_____
Daytime Telephone(____)_____